FOUR-SEASON
FOOD GARDENING

FOUR-SEASON FOOD GARDENING

How to grow vegetables, fruits, and herbs year-round

MISILLA DELA LLANA

COOL SPRINGS PRESS

First Published in 2022 by Cool Springs Press, an imprint of The Quarto Group,
100 Cummings Center, Suite 265-D, Beverly, MA 01915, USA.
T (978) 282-9590 F (978) 283-2742 QuartoKnows.com

26 25 24 23 22   1 2 3 4 5

ISBN: 978-0-7603-7273-9

Digital edition published in 2022
eISBN: 978-0-7603-7274-6

Library of Congress Control Number: 2021946885

Design: Allison Meierding
Photography (B = bottom, L = left, M = middle, R = right, T = top):
Alamy: 85T, 98TR, 160B
George Weigel: 22, 23, 44, 56, 78, 79TL, 79TR, 93, 96, 145
Janet Davis: 15RT, 47BR, 77, 155T, 182B
JLY Gardens: 14, 16L, 18, 19, 26, 27L, 27R, 30, 36BR, 38, 45BL, 48, 49, 52TL, 52BL, 53TL, 53BL, 60, 61, 62BR, 64TL, 64TR, 66, 70T, 70M, 73, 80, 81, 83BL, 84, 85BR, 86TL, 87, 88, 90, 91, 92TL, 92BR, 97TR, 97BR, 98TL, 98BL, 103BR, 104, 105, 108, 110BL, 112T, 114, 118, 123, 125, 127, 130, 135TR, 137, 140, 141, 144, 147, 148BL, 148BR, 156, 158, 161, 163, 164, 169, 170, 171T, 171B, 175, 178B, 180T, 180B
Melinda Myers: 15RB, 17T, 24, 134
Misilla dela Llana: 67BL, 70B, 103T, 122, 126TR, 150, 153BR, 154BR, 155B, 159, 160TL, 162, 165, 166, 172T, 173, 177, 179T, 181T, 181B, 182T, 183, 184
Shutterstock: 2, 6TL, 6TR, 6BL, 6BR, 7, 8LB, 8RB, 9RT, 10, 11, 12, 13TL, 13TR, 17B, 20, 21, 25, 28, 31, 32BL, 32BR, 35, 36T, 39, 41, 42, 43, 45BR, 46T, 46BR, 47BL, 50, 51, 54BL, 54BR, 55T, 55BR, 57, 58, 62BL, 63, 67TR, 67BR, 68, 69, 71, 72T, 72BL, 74, 75, 82, 83T, 86B, 89TL, 89BL, 92TR, 94, 99, 100, 102, 106, 107T, 107B, 109, 110TR, 110BR, 111T, 111B, 112B, 113, 115, 116, 119, 120, 121, 124, 126B, 128, 129T, 132, 133, 135TL, 138, 142, 143, 146T, 146B, 149TL, 149TR, 151, 152, 153BL, 154BL, 157, 167, 168, 172BR, 174, 176, 178T, 179B

Printed in China

DEDICATION

To my husband and our children, for all your love and support. To my mother, auntie, and uncle, for your continued guidance and encouragement. To my late father and grandfather, your passion for writing inspired me.

CONTENTS

INTRODUCTION

I spent my early childhood in the Philippines and have vivid recollections of the fruit trees that surrounded our home. Often food was scarce, but the trees provided us with succulent mangoes, although some were eaten immature as they were preferred for their crispy texture and tart, unripe fruit. Guava trees boasted sweet and pleasant berries that were eaten almost daily during the season. Banana plants were adjacent to our backyard, as well as coconuts from palm trees that naturally grew on the side of the dirt roads. When we moved to the States, my mother thoroughly enjoyed gardening, and I recall the flower beds cultivated with an array of vibrant tulips.

I remember the summer I picked a yellow pear tomato for the first time, and it was perfectly ripe and sweet! Our backyard was also home to a thicket of native Pacific blackberries. These prickly shrubs flourished with plump and juicy berries which were carefully handpicked every summer for mom to make jars of tangy-yet-sweet blackberry jam. One of my first summer jobs was picking blueberries at a local berry farm with my siblings and friends to earn money to buy school clothes and supplies. I thought then that the acres of various types of blueberries were amazing! Some berries had a diameter of a U.S. quarter, and a few were much smaller, but very tasty and sweet. Harvesting fruits at local farms later became a tradition with our own children. Autumns are spent picking apples, pears, stone fruits, and fall vegetables in my parents' backyard as well as at my aunt and uncle's property. The experience of seeing, harvesting, and tasting freshly picked food naturally instilled the value and importance of learning to grow my own edible landscape. A garden will not only give you fresh and nutritious food, but it's also a place for reconnecting with nature. Gardening promotes learning and empowerment. It is calming, good for the body and mind, and so much more.

Today I live in the beautiful Northwest, a temperate climate with four distinct yet subtle seasons

Left My mother always planted a garden consisting of vegetables, berries, herbs, and fruit trees. *Right* We plant several varieties of cold-hardy leafy greens such as kale, tatsoi, spinach, collards, and Swiss chard to help extend our harvest season.

Setting up season extenders is a handy way to lengthen your growing season.

influenced by the Pacific Ocean. Our maritime environment means a long spring with ample rain and a typically warm and dry summer. It's generally cool in winter, but it does not reach the extremes. Because of the moderate and mild seasons, it's safe to say that we can grow edible crops year-round, but we do require protection such as row covers in fall through early spring. However, I know that not all gardeners live in a similar climate. Because of this, growing a four-season vegetable garden will require more or less effort, depending on where you live. This book is meant to offer insight, ideas, and inspiration for ways you can grow edibles year-round, no matter what kind of climate you call home.

In the last few years, we have had more snow and colder days than usual, causing some hardy crops, including perennial tree collards, to perish during winter. A thick layer of mulch provides insulation, although long-standing snow on the ground and extremely cold temperatures may severely damage or even kill semi-hardy crops. I learned to apply certain methods in our backyard garden to shelter our crops and extend the harvest. This can be as simple as placing garden fabric over cool-weather crops planted in late summer. Doing so means additional harvests for a few weeks, even months, in temperate climates. Other options, such as a cold frame or an unheated greenhouse, can also provide some protection for winter-hardy vegetables. Throughout this book, you'll learn different techniques to extend your own growing season.

Besides showing you how to extend the harvest of annual vegetables, I'll introduce many hardy perennial crops that return to the garden reliably every year, even in very cold climates. By choosing the right crops, as well as incorporating perennials in a home garden, you'll have earlier harvests and greater yields once plants establish. Some of the permanent crops we grow include root and leafy vegetables, berries, and herbs, as well fruit trees. You'll learn more about these crops throughout this book.

Implementing season-extending techniques, growing different varieties of crops year-round, and integrating edible perennials will provide you and your family with bountiful harvests for years. My hope is to inspire you to cultivate and enjoy food grown organically while preserving soil health and the surrounding ecosystem.

1 PLANNING YOUR GARDEN

As you probably know, plants need sunlight, water, air, and fertile soil. Given ideal conditions, plants will thrive and produce. When selecting a location for your garden, make sure that you see it daily from inside your home. You're more likely to tend your garden when it's in sight. Avoid placing your garden at the bottom of a hill or any area where water collects and pools, especially after a rain; otherwise your garden will be at risk for flooding, which can cause problems. In this chapter, we'll look at these and many other factors you need to consider when deciding where to locate your garden.

To grow a successful garden, there are many factors to consider, including the area's sunlight exposure and what type of garden works best for the site.

SUNLIGHT

I recall celebrating Arbor Day in elementary school; each student was given a Douglas fir sapling. I planted the tiny tree right in front of our house. As a child, you don't usually think about the size of a tree at maturity. On average, a Douglas fir can grow 100–120 feet (30–37 m) tall, which would definitely cast shade on my mother's flower garden! I saw it grow over about four years to 5 feet (1.5 m) until we moved to another home nearby. Every few years I'll drive by our old house and have seen that tree grow to over 20 feet (6 m) tall.

The growth of towering evergreen trees obscures the sunlight over our property. Every year, our southwest area becomes shadier and cooler. We've changed things up a bit to accommodate the different requirements of plants as well as introduced new varieties that thrive in this microclimate.

Not all plants can adapt to climate shifts as growth can be hindered and may not be as vigorous as well as making them more vulnerable to pests and disease. This especially applies to crops requiring full sun such as tomatoes, peppers, squash, cucumber, and corn. All plants require sunlight to photosynthesize and grow. Through this process, plants utilize sunlight to convert light energy into chemical energy in the form of carbohydrates. As a result of photosynthesis, plants release exudates through their roots that feed microbes

A microclimate is a small region varying in atmospheric conditions from the surrounding area and can offer different growing environments. The brick walls around this garden hold heat and release it at night, creating a warmer microclimate for growing vegetables.

The rhizosphere is the area around a plant's root system. Microorganisms in the rhizosphere produce nutrients and plant hormones that support plant growth.

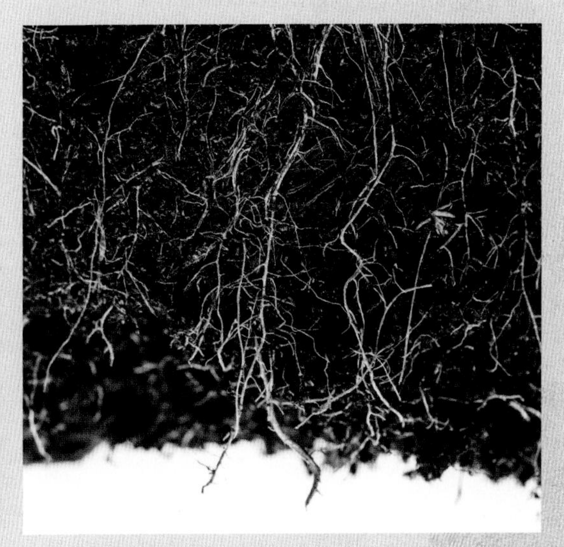

Through symbiosis between plants and microbes, sugars and amino acids known as exudates are secreted from plant roots, which become food for soil microorganisms.

such as fungi. Through this symbiotic relationship, fungi provide nutrients and water while hindering potentially harmful microbes in the rhizosphere (root zone).

Generally, plants thrive well in full sun, especially most vegetables, fruits, herbs, and flowers. However, some will flourish in part shade depending on the variety. Choosing the proper garden location will provide the essential needs of your plants and will result in healthy and productive crops.

The sun rises in the east and sets in the west but the rising and setting points change marginally every day. Overall, the sun moves from left to right, crossing from east to west with its highest point to the south, which is the ideal site for an edible landscape. Using a compass will help you determine the directions of your property and most, if not all, smartphones have a compass app you can download.

Full sun or half-day sun is at least 6 hours of direct sun daily, but to produce optimally many vegetables and fruits need 8–10 hours daily. Part-sun means a plant requires between 3–6 hours of direct sun per day; part-shade is 3–6 hours of sunlight but plants need shelter from intense afternoon sun. Plants that thrive in full shade require fewer than 3 hours of direct sun daily. When plotting a new planting site, it's a good idea to wait until surrounding trees leaf out. This will allow you to better observe the areas with the most daylight, allowing you to see parts that may be in shade cast by surrounding trees and other structures. On a sunny day, evaluate your property to monitor how much light each area receives; this can be broken into 1- to 2-hour intervals throughout the day. A section may get light exposure between 7–9, 10–12, and 1–4, which totals 7 hours. You can sketch your property, number the sections, and record the times when they get sun exposure.

The best areas usually receive full sun between 10 a.m.–5 p.m.; keep in mind that the strongest daylight is between 10 a.m.–2 p.m. If there are no obstacles surrounding your property, you have full contact with the sun during the day and will be able to plant your garden in that space. Not everyone has an open field, but by surveying and taking notes of the nearby surroundings that receive sufficient daylight, you will be able to plant your garden.

When selecting a location, make sure your garden faces south to receive the most daylight.

WATERING YOUR GARDEN

Water is just as essential to plants as sun, soil, and carbon dioxide. We receive an abundance of precipitation throughout the year although there are a few dry weeks during the warm summer. Dehydrated plants are unable to transport moisture, nutrients, and plant hormones where they're needed, which can halt growth and production and sometimes may kill your plants prematurely. Furthermore, inadequate watering leads to stressed plants, putting them at risk of disease and pest infestations. Whichever way you prefer to water, avoid wetting plant foliage, which may put them at increased risk of fungal diseases such as powdery mildew.

Ways to Water

Watering deep encourages plant roots to grow deep into the lower levels of the ground for moisture. Shallow and frequent watering is wasteful as it causes moisture to evaporate more quickly, which may lead to roots drying out between waterings and plant stress. Be sure to water all around the base of plants to reach the fibrous roots that grow near the surface. A nearby spigot will save time and labor. I prefer to water with watering cans and a garden hose, which I find therapeutic, and I get a nice little workout. Numerous watering can styles come in 1- to 2-gallon (3.8- to 7.4-L) capacities. Ones designed with two handles, one for carrying and the other for pouring, are much easier on the wrists and hands.

There are various types of nozzles with adjustable watering patterns. I prefer a heavy-duty nozzle constructed of metal, especially brass types that are more durable than plastic. They can withstand outdoor conditions and are much more resistant to corrosion. They are pricier but generally have a longer life.

It's not necessary to purchase a long garden hose. They are costlier, heavier, and can be difficult to move. If you need one longer than 50 feet (15 m), consider buying two and attach the extra one as needed. Longer hoses are also harder to drain when it's time to store them and will take up more space. A rubber hose is an excellent choice as they are long-lasting and durable. They are also more resistant to sun damage, cracking, and less likely to kink. Repetitive twisting and bending can shorten hose life and lead to splitting and cracking.

Deep watering promotes strong, healthy roots.

A rose attachment can provide a gentle shower, especially with newly planted beds, as seeds and seedlings can be dislodged and float away from a sudden douse of water.

A soaker hose is a great way to target irrigation water directly onto the roots of plants.

Many gardeners prefer and find it handy to either have a soaker hose set up or install drip irrigation. Both systems conserve water by having close contact with the soil and the base of plants for deep watering; therefore, water isn't wasted by running off surfaces or through evaporation as it gradually seeps through the systems' tiny holes, which can be set on timers. Soaker hoses are great for smaller gardens on level ground, are affordable, and easy to install. Both setups prevent water from getting onto the foliage of plants making them less subject to disease. For instructions on setting up a soaker hose, see page 19.

A 1,000 square-foot roof surface can yield 600 gallons of water from 1 inch of rainfall. Collect rainwater in BPA-free buckets or other containers that don't leach harmful substances.

A rain barrel can be installed to collect water runoff from the gutter system of your home. It can be attached to a downspout with a diverter. Several types and various sizes of barrels designed for accumulating rain can be purchased at many hardware stores.

COLLECTING RAINWATER

If your county or city permits the collection of rainwater, take advantage of this free and valuable resource. Harvesting rain is a great alternative to municipal or well water and can decrease water runoff to sewers, which carry fertilizers and other chemicals to local bodies of water. Rainwater is considered "soft water" as it doesn't contain chlorine, fluoride, or other elements. On the other hand, tap water is referred to as "hard water" as it's usually treated with chemicals and contains minerals and salts. Rainwater contains nitrates, which are a bioavailable form of nitrogen. Ammonia is also found in rainwater, which is converted by soil microbes such as fungi and bacteria into nitrites and then nitrates. This process is called "nitrification." Nitrogen is an essential macronutrient that plants need to flourish. Rainwater contains more oxygen than tap water.

According to the Environmental Protection Agency, most rainwater is slightly acidic and has a pH value of 5.0–5.5, which can free micronutrients such as iron, zinc, copper, and manganese that may be locked in soils having a higher pH value. In general, tap water has a pH range of 6.5–8.5, with anything over 7.0 being alkaline. Most vegetables thrive in slightly acidic to neutral soils (pH 6.5–7.0).

A cistern has a much higher price tag and will require professional installation. When choosing a rain barrel, consider the features and instructions noted in the sidebar on page 18.

Left If you receive lots of rain throughout the year, consider setting up a large tank or reservoir such as a cistern.

Below The atmosphere is comprised of 78 percent nitrogen. When it rains, nitrates and ammonium are carried along, usually after a thunderstorm. Based on numerous studies, lightning produces enough energy to split inert nitrogen gas molecules, which combine with oxygen to form nitrates, a form that plants can utilize.

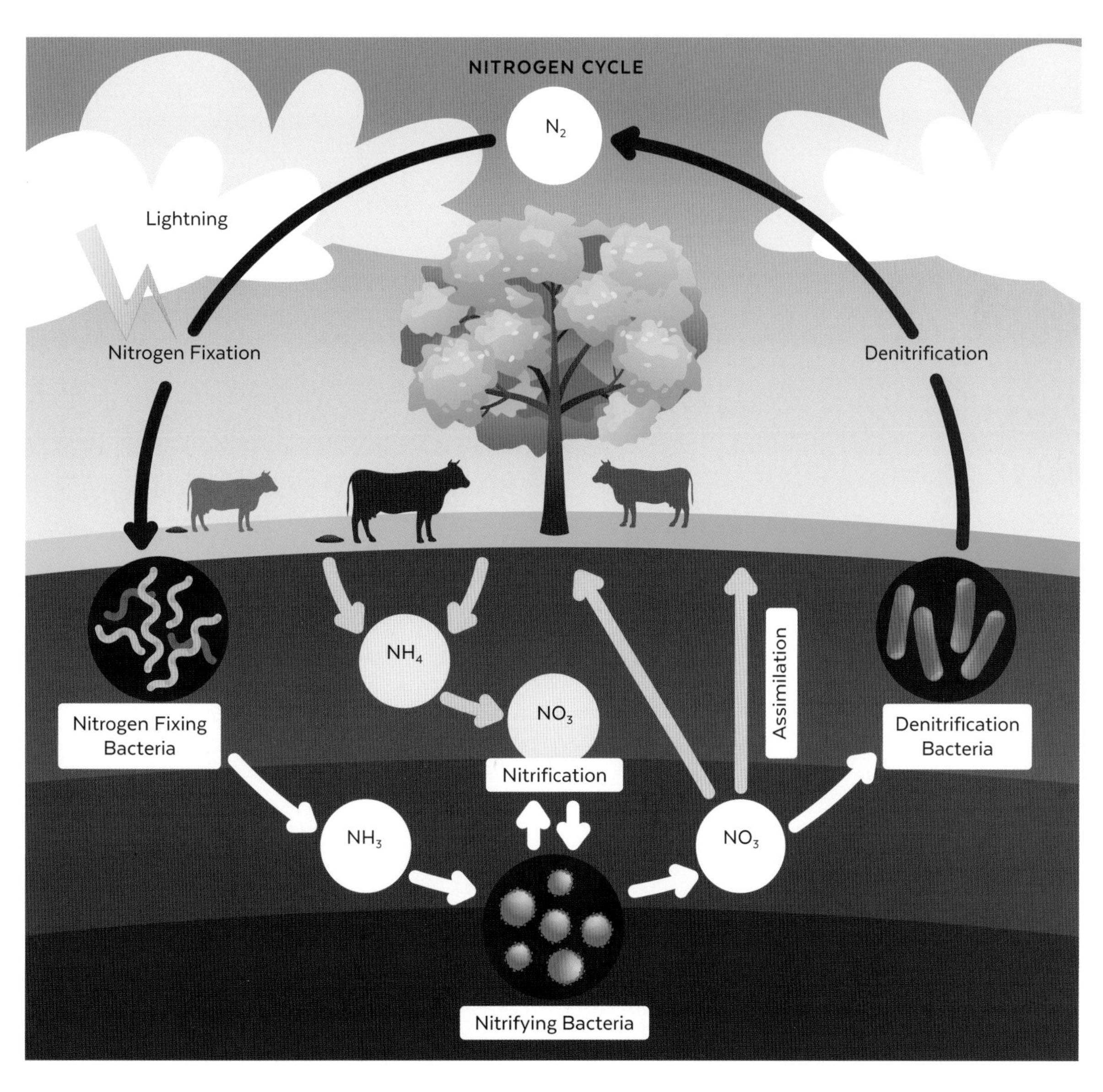

HOW TO SET UP A RAIN BARREL

- Spigot: For connecting a hose.
- Lid: Helps stop mosquitoes from breeding and allows you to scoop out water with a can or bucket.
- Screen: Keeps debris and animals out as well as insects such as mosquitoes. Mosquitoes may still be able to enter the barrel. If this occurs, try sprinkling granules of a biological mosquito control such as Bti (*Bacillus thuringiensis israelensis*). This soil-dwelling bacteria is used as a larvicide and works on fungus gnat larvae too.
- Some models are available in a collapsible form and others have flat backs for better use of space.

Read the instructions provided before installation. The gutters and downspouts of your home must be free of debris, in working condition, and there can be no electrical wires running through the downspout.

1. Select the gutter and downspout that you'll connect your barrel to. Prepare the area where the barrel will be stationed. Establish a level surface if you plan on placing it on the ground. Dig up about 1 inch (2.5 cm) of soil and put sand or gravel on the surface or use pavers to elevate it.
2. Place the barrel next to the downspout and cut the downspout so the barrel fits under it.
3. Attach a diverter to a section of the downspout; the diverter will connect a hose to the barrel. Then position it.
4. Some downspout diverters have an automatic overflow control to direct water back to the downspout when the barrel is full. Direct overflow *away* from your home's foundation. Consider securing the barrel to prevent it from falling over.
5. When not in use, disconnect and drain the barrel.

HOW TO SET UP A SOAKER HOSE

Soaker hoses work best on level ground or flat areas so the water is distributed evenly.

1. Unwind and leave any new soaker hoses out in the sun for about an hour to loosen the coil.
2. Remove the end cap and attach the hose to a water source. If more length is needed, connect the soaker hose to one end of another garden hose and attach that garden hose to the faucet.
3. Flush the soaker hose and run the water for a few minutes. (This can be done annually to remove debris.) Turn off the water.
4. Replace the end cap, straighten the hose, and turn on the water. Adjust the water valve until a slow and continuous drip begins.
5. If crops are planted on a straight line, place the soaker hose alongside the rows or snake the hose in and out for plants that are planted in staggered rows.
6. Loop the hose around plants that require more water.
7. Place 2–3 inches (5–7.5 cm) of mulch over the hose to prevent moisture loss. Use garden pins to secure the hose.

GARDEN TOOLS

Numerous gardening tools and pieces of equipment are on the market but aim for the basic ones that will get your tasks done. Choose high-quality tools that fit your budget and properly maintain and store them to increase their longevity. You'll avoid overcrowding storage space by focusing on *essential* tools. Store tools indoors to protect them from outdoor elements.

TOOLS AND THEIR PRIMARY FUNCTIONS

- **Garden Spade**: Digging, loosening, and breaking chunks of soil
- **Round Point Shovel**: Digging, transplanting, scooping, and building trenches
- **Rake**: Removing clods in the soil and smoothing surfaces
- **Garden Hoe**: Cutting down weeds and preparing garden beds
- **Hand Trowel**: Transplanting, planting in containers, and removing weeds
- **Garden Fork**: Digging and turning soil
- **Warren Hoe**: Deep cultivation such as tomatoes or sweet potatoes
- **Loppers**: Long-handled cutting tool for better reach and cutting thick branches
- **Pruning Shears**: Bypass pruners for live plants; anvil pruners for deadwood only
- **Wheelbarrow**: For heavy lifting and moving soil, compost, or mulch around the garden

TYPES OF GARDEN BEDS

Many gardeners successfully grow in native soil, raised beds, and containers. There are benefits and drawbacks to each so choose what works best for you. We started our garden in native soil with added amendments as well as in pots. Different areas of our property consist of rich clay, sandy soil, and loamy soil, which is the ideal structure. Clay drains slowly as its particles are tiny with the texture of flour and tend to bind together when wet. Clay soil has poor drainage and lacks permeability, which can cause plant roots to rot. Sandy soil will drain quickly but does not have the capacity to retain moisture and nutrients for extended periods.

Most of our growing spaces consist of raised beds, both framed and unframed, as well as containers. There are many benefits of raised beds, including improved soil structure that allows better drainage and porosity. They also warm and dry quicker. Raised beds make it possible to garden even if one has unsuitable or contaminated soil. A bed that's not enclosed (freeform) is basically native soil mounded above the soil grade into narrow beds, although it's subject to erosion and overflow. Framed beds prevent soil from washing away and require less room, especially important for anyone with limited space. A contained garden's height can be raised, making it convenient for people who have trouble bending and reaching. Framed and freeform beds can be any length with a recommended width of 2–4 feet (0.6–1.2 m)—or arm's length so you can reach and tend to crops planted near or at its center.

Raised beds can be constructed from wood, concrete blocks, logs, stones, galvanized steel, and other materials.

Depending on the materials you choose, set a budget and take advantage of any free resources. You can avoid investing more than is necessary when starting a new garden and can always expand later. Stay away from treated wood or other materials that may potentially leach chemicals into the soil and plants. There is a great selection of raised bed kits that can be easily assembled and set up for planting.

Unframed Raised Beds

An unframed raised bed is a narrow mound above soil grade. It's simple, sensible, and inexpensive. Here's how to set one up:

1. Select a sunny location with level ground and loamy soil.
2. Prepare the area by removing large rocks and plant debris.
3. The bed can be any length with a width of 2–4 feet (0.6–1.2 m).
4. Mound the bed with a 6-inch (15-cm) layer of organic compost or well-rotted manure and mix it into soil about 12 inches (30 cm) deep. Break up any clods to improve soil structure and water retention.
5. If any other soil amendment is needed, work it into the top 3–4 inches (7.5–10 cm) of the mound. Water the bed in gently using the spray setting on your hose's nozzle.
6. Wait a couple of weeks to allow the soil to settle and for the microorganisms to break down organic matter before planting.

Framed Raised Bed

Framed raised beds can be made of stone, wood, metal, bricks, or other materials. The design featured in the sidebar below uses cedar fence boards, which are practical and economical. It will last a few years longer than standard wood because cedar is hardy and less prone to rot and insects. These instructions are for a 3 feet by 3 feet (0.9 meters by 0.9 meters) bed with a depth of 11 inches (28 cm).

HOW TO BUILD A SIMPLE RAISED BED

- Four 6-foot untreated cedar fence boards with a 5½-inch (14-cm) width
- Two cedar deck balusters or one at 48 inches
- 3 dozen outdoor nails or deck screws (1⅝ inch, or 4 cm)
- Hammer
- Screwdriver or drill
- Saw
- Materials to fill bed (liner, soil, potting mix)

1. Choose a sunny area with level ground to build your raised bed.
2. Cut fence boards in half.
3. Cut deck balusters into 12-inch (30-cm) lengths.
4. Attach a baluster to one of the fence boards, ensuring the edges are flush. Secure the next fence board directly on top.
5. Secure the next 12-inch (30-cm) baluster on the opposite end, with edges flush. Repeat step 4 to build the opposite side.
6. Attach remaining boards to the sides to build your square. Stagger the height or angle of the screws or nails to prevent them from crossing.
7. Place the bed at your desired location. For aesthetics, feel free to add a trim or edging.
8. Line the bottom with cardboard; this will eventually decompose and add nutrients to the soil.
9. Fill bed with topsoil or landscaping fill, compost, and high-quality potting mix. A good ratio for a bed with a 12-inch (30-cm) depth is 25–30 percent compost, to 50 percent topsoil and 20–25 percent potting mix.
10. If you decide on a taller design (20 inches, or 50 cm, or more) a good way to save on soil is by implementing the Hügelkultur method. See the Hügelkultur sidebar on page 25.

Hügelkultur Mounds

We were first introduced to this method by our friends Gabe and Olivia. Their edible landscape consists of several Hügelkultur mounds whose foundation is built from dead wood, yard vegetation, and enriched with other organic materials. The hills are planted with an array of perennial crops including berry canes and shrubs, perennial collards, herbs, and garlic as well as culinary and medicinal mushrooms. Hügelkultur mounds can be cultivated with most edible or ornamental plants.

Taking advantage of available resources saves time, money, and labor. A few years ago, a friend told us about an organization that works closely with arborists in select regions. From them, I was able to acquire a truckload of free wood chips and logs delivered at no charge. Since then, our garden has been primarily covered with wood chips. Some logs were placed in the tall raised beds to fill the void at the bottom, which was more economical than filling them with compost and soil. The tall beds have a height of approximately 32 inches (81 cm). The word "hügelkultur" means "hill mound" or "hill culture", which entails mounding and layering biomass such as logs, branches, vegetation such as grass clippings and leaves, as well as kitchen scraps and cardboard. It consists of materials that you'd put in a compost heap with the addition of compost or finished manure. After the layers of organic matter are placed, it's topped with organic compost and planting soil. The materials below decay over time, returning nutrients to the soil while the logs and branches retain moisture like sponges, which is released over dry periods. The logs and branches generate heat during decomposition, prolonging the growing season. Hügelkultur is known to sequester carbon and store it in the mound.

Hügelkultur mounds last about 5–6 years and must be rebuilt from scratch. This practice is often used in permaculture gardens.

Hügelkultur is a sustainable horticultural method that has been applied in Germany and Eastern Europe for hundreds of years.

HOW TO BUILD A HÜGELKULTUR BED

1. Find a sunny location and test the soil for possible contaminants before starting a mound. Remove the sod, and dig a trench with a depth of 12–18 inches (30.5–45.7 cm) deep.
2. Lay dead wood lengthwise though the center, reaching both ends with a height of 2 feet (60 cm).
3. Layer more woody debris such as sticks, branches, and yard trimmings (including the sod). Ensure the pile is tapered to the ground on all sides. Use a shovel to pound and shape the mound and to smooth the surface.
4. Add another layer of dead vegetation and garden soil along with some finished manure.
5. Layer organic compost and soil on top and shape the hill using a shovel.
6. Hügelkultur beds need time to break down before planting. Start a mound in fall for a spring garden. As the materials decompose, it will settle to around 2 feet (60 cm) tall.

Note: Do not use treated wood, black walnut, black locust, or redwood heartwood.

Containers come in a wide variety of styles and sizes that suit a gardener's preferences, from fancy ceramic to classic terracotta pots.

Container Gardening

Our first garden was on the balcony of our condominium. We mainly grew herbs, tomatoes, lettuce, and strawberries. Growing in containers has several advantages especially for people with limited growing space, and it's a great option if you have poor soil conditions.

Place planters on decks, balconies, driveways, and patios and move them to different areas where adequate sunlight exposure exists. Situate large pots on plant dollies or caddies with wheels for easy transport. Use quality potting soil that's comprised of vital nutrients and organic matter, has good moisture retention, drains well, and is porous. Containers require consistent fertilization and irrigation as some nutrients wash away each time the plants are watered, and they dry out faster than raised or in-ground beds. Container plants may require fertilization every 2 weeks, depending on what you're growing, and should be watered as necessary. If you're not sure when to water, stick your finger into the top 1 inch (2.5 cm) of the soil: if it's dry, water until it drains out through the holes. Avoid getting water on plant foliage, which can lead to fungal diseases such as powdery mildew. Whether you decide to plant in a refurbished horse trough, hanging baskets, or fabric pots, you can have success as long your plants' growing requirements are met.

A vertical grow tower is practical and a great option for small spaces. They sometimes come with a caddy so it can be easily moved.

Fence planters, fabric grow pouches, and window box containers placed on top of railings are more ways to grow vertically.

VERTICAL CONTAINER GROW TOWERS

Multiple stacks of containers allow you to grow several varieties of vegetables, herbs, or flowers. Some are equipped with a water reservoir at the top for irrigation or for fertilization. Depending on where you station your grow tower, rotate it 180 degrees every other day so that sunlight is evenly distributed among the plants. Crops that we've grown in a garden tower include strawberries, bush beans, radish, baby carrots, leafy greens, garlic, and scallions as well as herbs.

TERRACOTTA POTS

Woody Mediterranean herbs such as rosemary, sage, thyme, and lavender thrive in clay pots due to the pots' porous nature. These herbs prefer lean sandy loam soil that drains well as they don't like wet roots. Woody herbs are drought tolerant, and their soil can be left to dry between waterings once they're established. If you plan to grow herbaceous herbs such as basil, cilantro, chives, or parsley in terracotta pots, plan to water and fertilize them more frequently than you do woody herbs.

Fabric pots have become extremely popular for home gardens.

CHOOSING THE RIGHT SIZE CONTAINERS

When selecting containers, make sure they are large enough to support the growth and development of the plants. Check labels or seed packets for a plant's anticipated mature size. Pots that are too small and shallow will not allow sufficient room for root expansion, can dry out rather quickly, and can stunt plant growth. Plants with deep root systems, such as tomato, pumpkin, and globe artichoke, should be grown in taller containers.

FABRIC CONTAINERS

Fabric pots are typically made of a lightweight and breathable material such as woven or non-woven polypropylene, which is similar to landscaping fabric. They come in an assortment of colors and sizes ranging from less than a gallon (4.6 liters) to as large as a raised bed. Their portability makes them easier to set up before soil is added. Fabric pots are a great alternative to traditional containers as their permeable structure allows excellent ventilation. When plant roots are exposed to oxygen, root tips naturally prune themselves; this is known as air pruning. This process stimulates plants to constantly produce new, healthy branching roots. A fibrous root structure is more efficient as it can take in moisture and nutrients within a larger area including near the surface. Air pruning prevents roots from circling around inside the pot, which leads to rootbound plants.

On the following page is a table of suggested container sizes for specific plant types. Leafy greens such as lettuce can be grown closely (intensive planting) and harvested with the cut-and-come-again method.

Once you have determined how you'd like to begin your garden—whether in-ground, in containers, or in raised beds—the next chapter will cover how to build healthy soil. You will learn about soil structure, organic amendments that will create proper soil consistency, and establishing soil fertility. Your soil's composition is the key element to support what you intend to grow and will establish the foundation for productive yields.

CONTAINER SIZE CHART

PLANT	DIAMETER	VOLUME	NUMBER OF PLANTS
Arugula	8-9 inches (20-23 cm)	1-2 gallons (3.8-7.6 L)	4-6 plants
Basil	8-9 inches (20-23 cm)	2 gallons (7.6 L)	3-4 plants
Bean (Bush)	12 inches (30 cm)	5 gallons (19 L)	4 plants
Blueberry	12 inches (30 cm) for young plants; 24-30 inches (60-75cm) for mature plants	5 gallons (19 L) for young plants; 25-30 gallons (94-114 L) for mature plants	1 plant
Broccoli	12 inches (30 cm)	5 gallons (19 L)	1 plant
Bunching Onions	6-8 inches (15-20 cm)	1 gallon (3.8 L)	3-6 bulbs
Carrot	12 inches (30 cm)	5 gallons (19 L)	12-14 plants
Chard	12 inches (30 cm)	5 gallons (19 L)	2-3 plants
Chives	6-8 inches (15-20 cm)	1 gallon (3.8 L)	8-10 bulbs
Cilantro	8-9 inches (20-23 cm	1-2 gallons (3.8-7.6 L)	3-4 plants
Collards	12 inches (30 cm)	5 gallons (19 L)	1 plant
Cucumber	12 inches (30 cm)	5 gallons (19 L); 10-15 gallons (38-56 L) for vining	1 plant (compact)
Eggplant	12 inches (30 cm)	5 gallons (19 L)	1 plant
Garlic	12 inches (30 cm)	5 gallons (19 L)	6 cloves spaced 4 inches apart
Kale	12 inches (30 cm)	5 gallons (19 L)	1 plant
Leaf Lettuce	12 inches (30 cm)	5 gallons (19 L)	4-5 plants
Lettuce	12 inches (30 cm)	5 gallons (19 L)	1-2 plants
Mint	6-8 inches (15-20 cm)	1-2 gallons (3.8-7.6 L)	1 plant (consider window boxes as it spreads sideways)
Onion	12 inches (30 cm)	5 gallons (19 L)	4-5 plants
Oregano	6-8 inches (15-20 cm)	1-2 gallons (3.8-7.6 L)	1 plant
Parsley	6-8 inches (15-20 cm)	1-2 gallons (3.8-7.6 L)	1-2 plants
Pepper	12 inches (30 cm)	5 gallons (19 L)	1 plant
Pumpkin (Small)	16-18 inches (40-46 cm)	15 gallons (56 L)	1 plant
Pumpkin (Large)	21-24 inches (53-61 cm)	20-25 gallons (78-95 L)	1 plant
Radish	12 inches (30 cm)	5 gallons (19 L)	12 plants
Rosemary	12 inches (30 cm)	5 gallons (19 L)	1 plant
Spinach	12 inches (30 cm)	5 gallons (19 L)	4-6 plants
Strawberry	10 inches (25.5 cm)	3 gallons (11 L)	1 plant
Summer Squash	14-16 inches (35-40 cm)	10-15 gallons (38-56 L)	1 plant
Thyme	8-9 inches (20-23 cm)	1-2 gallons (3.8-7.6 L)	1-2 plants
Tomato (Micro-dwarf, determinate 6-9 inches, or 15-23 cm, tall)	6-8 inches (15-20 cm)	1-2 gallons (3.8-7.6 L)	1 per 1- to 2-gallon (3.8- to 7.6-L) pot
Tomato (Determinate)	18 inches (46 cm)	15 gallons (56 L)	1 plant
Tomato (Indeterminate)	21-24 inches (53-61 cm)	20-25 gallons (78-95 L)	1 plant

2

SOIL AND FERTILITY

When I first started my gardening journey, I didn't pay much attention to continually fertilizing the container garden on our balcony. I figured a bag of potting mix and watering consistently was enough. I was disappointed when our tomatoes and strawberries prematurely halted production and lost vigor in midsummer due to nutrient deficiency. For crops to thrive and produce, we must first build a foundation to support and sustain development and production. Plants require a steady supply of nutrients and water to flourish. Inadequate nourishment can lead to slow or stunted growth as well as increased vulnerability to pests and disease.

Sand, silt, and clay bind together to form varying masses of soil or aggregates. A good soil texture can hold its shape when molded together but should slowly come apart when you squeeze it out of your hand. You can perform a ribbon test by feeling the consistency of your native soil (see page 32).

Humus is dark organic material produced from decaying plant and animal matter that's been broken down by soil microorganisms; think of the soil found on a forest floor. What makes humus such an essential soil component is its ability to preserve fertility by holding onto nutrients and water. Further, humus supports and houses soil microbes in its tiny nooks and crannies that break down nutrients, making them bioavailable for plant uptake. In addition, humus may assist in suppressing plant diseases by extracting harmful bacteria and fungi or toxins in the soil. In this chapter, we'll look at ways you can improve your soil and ensure your plants have adequate nutrition for optimum growth.

A loamy soil is composed of the right balance of sand, silt, clay, some organic matter, and humus, which makes a perfect soil structure.

SOIL RIBBON TEST

1. Scoop a small handful of soil about 3 inches (7.6 cm) below the soil surface.
2. Place the soil on a pan or cookie sheet and remove rocks and plant debris such as roots.
3. Break up the clumps of aggregates, if any, using a wooden spoon or spatula.
4. Dampen the soil with water, a little at a time, until its consistency feels like wet Play-doh.
5. Roll into a ball, about 1½ inches (3.5 cm) in diameter.
6. Slowly squeeze the ball of soil between your thumb and forefinger until it forms a ribbon.
7. The weight of the soil will break the ribbon into 1- to 2-inch (2.5- to 5-cm) lengths or longer.
8. If the ribbon is 1 inch (2.5 cm) long and does not feel sandy or gritty, then it's loam soil.
9. If the ribbon is 2 inches (5 cm) or longer, and feels smooth and sticky, then it's comprised mainly of clay. Remember, clay particles are much smaller than sand and silt, giving it a smooth texture; clay soil does not drain well.
10. A loam soil is comprised of mainly sand, silt, and clay. A typical ratio will have about 40 percent sand, 40 percent silt, and 20 percent clay.

MICROBE POWER

Microbes play a vital role in soil health and fertility. A teaspoon of rich fertile soil can contain 100 million to 1 billion bacteria—isn't that amazing? The nutrients found in soil are manufactured by micro- and macrofauna including fungi, bacteria, and protozoa as well as earthworms, arthropods, mollusks, and nematodes, which all contribute to soil life and fertility known as the soil food web.

DIY SOIL COMPOSITION TEST IN A JAR

1. Use a trowel to dig 12 inches (30 cm) into the ground.
2. Fill a quart glass jar halfway with soil. (Use a screen or sieve to remove debris and large particles such as rocks.)
3. Add water to the jar, filling it three-quarters full; add 1 teaspoon dish soap.
4. Secure with a lid and shake about 3 minutes.
5. Set the jar aside to settle for 48 hours.
6. You'll notice sand particles at the very bottom, followed by silt, then clay, which is the lightest in weight and has the smallest fragments. If you see a sediment with three layers like the ratio described, this is a good loam soil. The water on top should remain clear. Loam soil drains well, retains moisture and nutrients, and has good porosity.
7. If the water is murky with a thin layer of particles, you have clay soil. Clay soil does not drain well and can cause waterlogged roots.
8. Sandy soil results in one layer of sandy particles at the bottom and the water will be clear. This soil structure drains well but will not hold nutrients and moisture for extended periods.

TESTING SOIL DRAINAGE AND FERTILITY

Before cultivating native soil, perform this simple technique to test drainage and soil life. You'll have results within an hour.

1. Select a planting area and dig a square hole to a depth of 12 inches (30 cm).
2. Place the excavated soil on a mound next to the hole and carefully inspect it for earthworms.
3. If you find 8–12 worms, that's a good sign of a moderately fertile soil.
4. To check drainage, fill the hole with water three-quarters of the way.
5. If the hole completely drains within an hour, it drains well.
6. If it does not drain within an hour, consider a new location or construct a raised bed above soil grade instead. Poorly draining soil will only lead to problems in the future.

SOIL pH

Soil pH measures the alkalinity or acidity on a scale of 1–14, with 7 being neutral. Higher numbers mean the soil is more alkaline and lower numbers indicate more acidity.

In the Pacific Northwest, our soil is slightly acidic with a pH of 5.0–5.5. While favorable to acid-loving plants such as blueberries, most vegetables thrive in a soil pH between 6–7. If the soil is out of balance, nutrients can "lock up," preventing plants from acquiring the necessary nutrients to grow. If your soil falls on the acidic side, you can amend it with dolomitic lime, which contains calcium and magnesium carbonate and will raise the pH. You can find simple soil test kits at most garden centers, hardware stores, or online. I send my soil samples to a laboratory for accuracy and a complete analysis of nutrients and pH, as well as to check for potential contamination. The testing lab provides recommendations of amendments to fix any soil shortages.

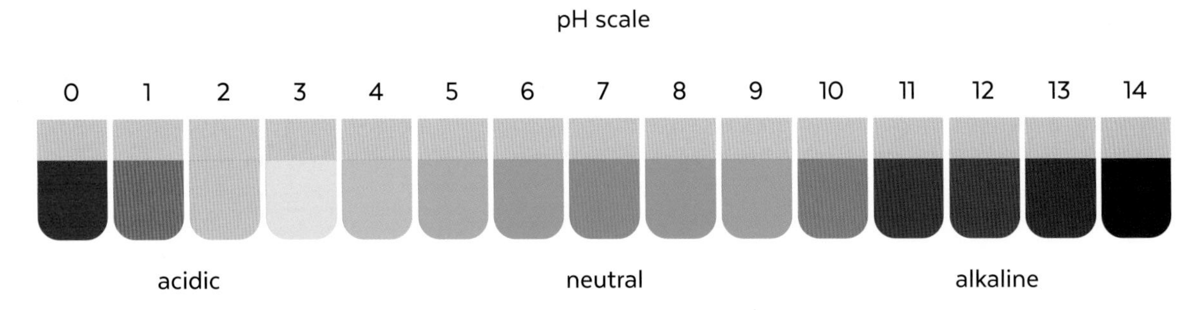

The pH in different parts of your garden can vary; it's wise to take samples from other sites.

SOIL NUTRIENTS

There are thirteen vital plant nutrients, broken into three groups: primary, secondary, and micronutrients. The three primary macronutrients plants need are nitrogen, phosphorus, and potassium. Nitrogen is a key component of chlorophyll, the compound plants utilize to produce food (sugars) from carbon dioxide and water through photosynthesis. Chlorophyll gives plants their green color and supports vegetative growth. Nitrogen is essential in the formation of amino acids or protein synthesis. Phosphorus assists root growth and flower, fruit, and seed production, as well as maintaining plant health. Potassium helps move water, carbohydrates, and nutrients within the plant tissue. It strengthens roots, reduces water loss, and builds a plant's resistance to diseases. Potassium contributes to protein synthesis and aids in setting fruit and seed production as well as increasing crop yields. Secondary nutrients include calcium, which supports cell walls, sulfur, a constituent of proteins, and magnesium, which supports photosynthesis. Listed in the table are seven micronutrients that plants use in tiny amounts, which are usually sufficient in fertile soil.

PLANT NUTRIENTS

Primary Nutrients
- Nitrogen (N)
- Phosphorus (P)
- Potassium (K)

Secondary Nutrients
- Calcium (Ca)
- Magnesium (Mg)
- Sulfur (S)

Micronutrients
- Boron (B)
- Chlorine (Cl)
- Copper (Cu)
- Iron (Fe)
- Manganese (Mn)
- Molybdenum (Mo)
- Zinc (Zn)

N-P-K Ratios

The N-P-K ratio stands for the percentage of each nutrient by volume. For example, a 10-10-10 fertilizer contains 10 percent nitrogen, 10 percent phosphorus, and 10 percent potassium. A 5-0-0 fertilizer contains 5 percent nitrogen but does not contain phosphorus or potassium, and it's considered incomplete. Getting your soil tested will help you determine if you need to add certain nutrients.

Organic versus Synthetic Fertilizers

Conventional or inorganic fertilizers are frequently used by commercial growers. They are commonly produced from byproducts of the petroleum industry as well as added minerals. They are available in dry forms such as granules and water-soluble products. While synthetic fertilizers are fast-acting, over time they can cause salt build up, deplete the soil of nutrients, and harm soil microorganisms. Overusing chemical fertilizers may allow chemicals to leach deep into the soil and water table and produce runoff to bodies of water.

Organic fertilizers are environmentally friendly and are generally sourced from plants, animal wastes, and minerals. These amendments are in slow-release forms, which take time to break down with the assistance of macro- and microorganisms in the soil. Organic fertilizers not only add essential nutrients, but they also enhance soil structure to improve water flow and capacity. Using natural amendments fosters healthy soil ecosystems, doesn't promote salt build-up, and doesn't release harmful chemicals in the ground.

SOIL AMENDMENTS

If you decide to plant in native soil, test it for possible contaminants and consider performing the simple soil structure test I've described. You can utilize the free resources at your local government or university agricultural office. Depending on the outcomes, you may have to condition your soil accordingly.

Adding organic compost or well-rotted manure can enhance the overall profile both of clay and sandy soils. With a little patience, this can be achieved in a few years. Let's talk about a few amendments you might use to improve your garden soil.

Right To aerate the soil, push a garden fork about 8–12 inches (20–30 cm) into the ground, move it forward and then toward you, move to the next section, and repeat. This task can be achieved more easily using a broad fork that has tines about twice as long and about three times wider than a garden fork.

Spread about 3-4 inches (7.5-10 cm) of finished compost on top of new garden beds, break up any clods, and smooth it with a rake. The ratio is 25-30 percent organic material to a bed with a 12-inch (30-cm) depth.

Compost

Compost is a dark crumbly material that has an earthy smell. It's produced from decomposing organic matter, such as woody materials, dead leaves, and grass, that's broken down by microorganisms that naturally occur outdoors. Compost is rich in nutrients, humus, and beneficial microbes. Adding compost to garden soil can improve drainage and porosity, help it resist soil compaction and erosion, and aid nutrient and moisture retention. Compost will continue to break down through soil microbial activity and release nutrients over time. Add only finished compost that does not contain pieces of un-decomposed matter as decomposition releases heat and can harm plants. Any carbon matter that has not been completely broken down can temporarily rob plants of nitrogen.

Manures

Manure is produced from decayed animal droppings and possesses benefits similar to compost. It improves soil fertility and structure and prevents soil erosion. Manure also contains microorganisms. Animal manures can be derived from poultry, cattle, horse, and rabbit as well as earthworms.

Worm Castings

Worm castings, aka worm poo, is a natural nutrient-dense fertilizer. It consists of essential macro- and micronutrients, beneficial microbes such as fungi and bacteria, humus, and plant hormones. Worm castings prevent soil runoff, compaction, and crusting while enhancing water-holding capacity and aeration and retaining nutrients.

Bloodmeal

Bloodmeal is dried and powdered animal blood, a byproduct of the meat industry. It's a good source of nitrogen, an especially important macronutrient necessary for plant growth and development.

Bonemeal

Bonemeal is another byproduct of the meat industry. It is derived from animal bones that are crushed into granules or powdered. Bone meal is rich in phosphorus and calcium and has traces of nitrogen.

Fish Meal

Fish meal is made from bones and offal, which are the parts not used by the commercial fishing industry. Fish meal contains essential nutrients and provides food for soil microfauna.

Kelp Meal

Kelp meal is dehydrated seaweed that can be processed into meal, powdered, or converted to liquid. Kelp meal typically has a low N-P-K value but it's an excellent source of micronutrients and plant growth hormones, plus it enhances soil composition, which increases crop yields. Kelp meal can be used as a topdressing or soil conditioner, although it needs time to break down before nutrients are accessible for plant uptake, which can take up to four months. The powder and liquid concentrate are good options as the nutrients are readily available.

Alfalfa Meal

Alfalfa is a perennial leguminous plant. Alfalfa meal is dried alfalfa that has been ground and pelletized. Like most legumes, alfalfa is a nitrogen-fixing plant. It's a beneficial soil conditioner comprised of nitrogen, phosphorus, potassium, and trace minerals, plus it contains a plant hormone that assists photosynthesis. Alfalfa meal can be used as a compost activator for its nitrogen and protein content, which heat organic matter to speed decomposition.

Lime

Lime is used as a soil amendment for raising the pH level, which makes soil less acidic. It's obtained from limestone. Dolomitic types contain calcium carbonate and magnesium carbonate. Calcitic types contain only calcium carbonate.

Azomite

Azomite is a volcanic ash also known as rock dust that's mined in central Utah. Azomite provides trace elements and micronutrients, especially for depleted soil. It's said that this ash was ejected from an ancient volcanic eruption.

Elemental Sulfur

Elemental sulfur is applied to lower the soil pH around acid-loving plants such as most berries and citrus trees that prefer acidic soil. Lowering the pH helps unlock nutrients necessary for growth and development.

COMPOSTING AT HOME

Composting is good for the environment as it reduces landfill waste, decreases greenhouse gas emissions, and is great for our gardens. Composting also allows you to grow nutritious food for less money! Finished compost adds humus and nutrients to the soil and enhances soil texture. This ecofriendly resource improves the capacity for water and nutrient retention as well as aeration and drainage. Additionally, compost introduces essential soil microbes that assist in the decomposition of organic matter, thus making nutrients bioavailable for plant uptake. Yard wastes such as plant trimmings, grass clippings, and leaves as well as kitchen scraps consisting of vegetables, fruits, eggshells, tea bags, and coffee grounds can be turned into compost, aka "black gold," in a few months.

You can start a pile on the ground, use a compost tumbler, and even start a worm-composting bin. Whichever method you choose with a little patience and determination you'll be rewarded with a natural and nutrient-dense soil enhancer while lessening your reliance on store-bought synthetic fertilizers.

Homemade compost is "black gold" to a gardener.

Making Compost

A compost tumbler is completely sealed with the exception of aeration holes, and it is rotated to mix the contents inside. It retains more heat from the process which speeds up decomposition and you can have finished compost in as little as 3–4 weeks. A less expensive method to contain your pile can be achieved with a wire fence or by building a simple wood box, although it will take a little longer to finish, or if you prefer, you can build a heap on the ground.

Making compost requires organic materials, water, heat, and macro- and microorganisms. To make compost, you'll need to collect green and brown materials, which are nitrogen and carbon sources, as well as organic matter such as compost, manure, or garden soil, which will introduce microbes. Nitrogen sources include kitchen scraps, *fresh* grass clippings and yard trimmings, as well as spent coffee grounds and tea. Eggshells can be added, even though they don't contribute to the nitrogen and carbon they are a good source of calcium, which contributes to the formation of plant cell walls. I suggest adding eggshells only to an enclosed bin or tumbler, as they attract rodents.

Carbon materials include straw, hay, dry leaves and dried lawn clippings, wood chips, shredded paper, and cardboard pieces. Each time you place a layer, water it in; a compost pile should have a moisture content between 40–60 percent. A pile that is too dry will slow microbial activity and if it's too wet, it can become anaerobic and give off a foul smell. Build your heap at least 3 feet high (0.9 meters) and wide to speed decomposition. The center of the mound will generate heat from the microorganisms decomposing the pile, assuming there's a good ratio of ingredients. Do not add pet waste or diseased plants; not all pathogens are eliminated and some may survive. Some disease pathogens are killed in temperatures above 135 F. You can compost year-round, but decomposition slows during cool seasons.

LAYERING THE MATERIALS

1. Select a location with level ground in a sunny area. Make sure it drains well.
2. Start with a 3- to 4-inch (7.5- to 10-cm) layer of brown materials.
3. Add 3–4 inches (7.5–10 cm) of greens.
4. Top it off with 1–2 inches (2.5–5 cm) of soil, manure, or compost.
5. Water each layer as you add it, until it is the consistency of a wrung-out towel.
6. The center of the pile should heat up by day 4 and could reach as high as 160°F (71°C).
7. When the heap cools, turn the pile so the center is rotated to the outer edges; this incorporates air and promotes even heating.
8. Turn your pile every other day. The more frequently you turn, the faster it will break down. You can have finished compost in 3–4 months.
9. The finished product should be dark brown like coffee grounds with a crumbly texture and earthy smell.
10. Apply a ¼- to ½-inch (0.6- to 1-cm) layer as a topdressing or work it into the soil. For new beds add 3–4 inches (7.5–10 cm) or 25–30 percent ratio for beds with a 12-inch (30-cm) depth. For established beds add 1–2 inches (7.5–10 cm).
11. If you'd rather save your energy for other tasks and not turn your pile so frequently, let nature do its thing; the pile will break down over time. This may take 1–2 years depending on materials used and your climate.

The bottomless wire bin shown can be filled by layering green and brown materials.

FOLIAR FEEDING

Nutrients are readily delivered by foliar feeding, and this works effectively for plants facing nutrient deficiencies or stress. You can use compost or worm castings tea as a foliar spray or purchase formulated liquid fertilizers. The nutrients are sprayed on plant leaves and are absorbed via leaf stomata, which are essentially pores located in a leaf's epidermis. Most stomata are on the undersides of leaves but spraying the top sides is beneficial as well.

Foliar feeding is more efficient when done before 10 a.m. when the stomata are open so nutrients are easily taken in. Avoid spraying in direct sunlight as the leaves can burn. Apply as a supplemental feeding once a week or every two weeks. Plants will still require nutrients from the soil. Compost and/or worm castings tea can also be applied as a soil drench.

CROP ROTATION

Crop rotation is a practice where the location of each crop changes each garden season. This is to maintain soil fertility, thus hindering the depletion of nutrients. It also maintains healthy soil and microbial populations as well reduces the development of plant diseases and insect damage. When a certain crop is planted at the same location over several years, it has a higher exposure to pathogens that proliferate on a specific plant or plant family.

This also relates to insect pests that tend to return or linger if a host plant remains at the same location. Rotating crops not only reduces plant vulnerability, but it can also replenish soil nutrients as each plant type utilizes only what it requires, balancing nutrient loss and giving the soil time to recover. The list below shows each family of vegetables that can be rotated in different plots or planting rows over a duration of 4 years.

FIRST YEAR

- Nightshade family: tomato, pepper, potato, eggplant
- Legume family: peas, beans
- Brassica family: Kale, radish, cabbage, bok choy
- Carrot family: parsley, carrot, parsnip, cilantro

SECOND YEAR

- Carrot family
- Nightshade family
- Legume family
- Brassica family

THIRD YEAR

- Brassica family
- Carrot family
- Nightshade family
- Legume family

FOURTH YEAR

- Legume family
- Brassica family
- Carrot family
- Nightshade family

Properly managed and well-prepared soil is labor saving and allows you to save time and be resourceful in setting up season extenders to prolong your growing period. The next chapter will discuss different techniques and skills that can be applied to your home garden for a longer and more rewarding season.

3
EXTENDING THE SEASON

A few years ago, my mother gave me a bay laurel that had been propagated from her tree. After a few weeks of nurturing, I transplanted it into my garden near a fence. This location receives full sun and the soil was suitable for this Mediterranean native. I figured the fence would provide a barrier from strong winds in fall and winter. Adjacent to it is a pile of large rocks that absorb the sun's energy during the day and release heat at night, giving the bay laurel a more sheltered environment in which to grow. Small, favorable environments like these are known as microclimates and making good use of them is the best way to extend your growing season. In this chapter, I'll share more information about microclimates, how to create them, and tips for maximizing your growing season.

Microclimates, such as the one created beneath the cover of this mobile raised bed, are useful for extending the growing season.

MICROCLIMATES

A microclimate is a small area with its own unique climatic conditions. These specific locations have variations in sunlight exposure, temperature, moisture, and wind. Structures such as buildings, concrete walls, and patios as well as nearby bodies of water contribute to differing atmospheric conditions. In home gardens, these areas can provide favorable growing environments for several types of crops.

Buildings, trees, fences, and other structures provide shade at different times throughout the day, making them the perfect spot for vegetables that thrive in dappled or part-shade (4-6 hours of sunlight daily).

Concrete, Rock Walls, and Hedges

The ability of concrete or rock walls to absorb heat during the day points to a good location for a raised bed or a container garden for planting cool-season crops in spring, fall, and through winter. The wall captures and stores heat energy from the sun during the day, which is then released at night to surrounding areas; this is referred to as "thermal mass." Heat-loving crops such as tomatoes, eggplants, and peppers grown in temperate climates benefit from this later in the season as heat is distributed to aid the ripening process. Garden fabric or row cover placed over cool-season crops can prolong a harvest through winter in moderate climates as the cover traps warmth. Concrete and stone walls can act as windbreakers to protect plants from harsh weather conditions. The same can be applied to masonry structures and boulders. While evergreen hedges serve as privacy walls, they can also shelter crops from outdoor elements.

Soil-based Microclimates

The variations of soil structure throughout your property may produce characteristics of microclimates as well. In full-sun places consisting of dry

Walls, walkways, and even hedges can create microclimates in a garden.

or lean soil, consider growing drought-tolerant Mediterranean herbs such as rosemary, sage, thyme, or lavender. If you have consistently moist soil in a shady location, try growing miner's lettuce (claytonia), which thrives in full or part shade and in moist soil. Numerous edible crops will flourish below tree canopies especially during dry and hot summers. Cultivate areas with existing microclimates and choose the right crops to prolong your growing season throughout the year. For a list of shade-tolerant herbs, see page 53.

Mulch

Mulch creates a microclimate when a layer of material is placed on the soil's surface. Mulch conserves moisture and prevents soil from eroding. Uncovered soil tends to develop a crust, which can obstruct water from filtering through the ground. Mulch regulates soil temperature, insulates plant roots in fall and winter, and keeps roots cool in summer. This practice also protects soil micro-organisms, which maintain fertility and can reduce weed proliferation. Over time, layers of organic mulch degrade to provide food for microbes and other soil organisms, recycling nutrients back into the soil. Moreover, it is aesthetically appealing. We normally use wood chips, dry grass clippings, and fall leaves to cover the surfaces of our garden beds and containers. We try to be resourceful by using what we have on hand and are fortunate to have a wonderful neighbor who shares his grass clippings and fall leaves adjacent to our planting site! You may be able to acquire free wood chips from a local arborist.

WHEN AND HOW TO APPLY MULCH

Upon the arrival of spring, wait to mulch until the soil warms. Applying too soon will maintain low soil temperatures, which can hinder plant growth. Before placing a layer of organic material, remove weeds and water deeply if the soil is dry. Depending on the type of organic material, place a 1- to 4-inch (2.5- to 10-cm) layer of mulch over the surface of the soil; a thicker layer may block oxygen. Keep mulch away from foliage. Mulch may be applied again in late fall before the first hard freeze to protect perennial crops.

TYPES OF ORGANIC MULCH

- Finished compost
- Woodchips
- Dry grass clippings
- Straw
- Hay
- Shredded fall leaves
- Pine needles
- Bark
- Coconut coir
- Sawdust

Apply organic mulch a few inches away from the base of plants to prevent moisture build-up, which can lead to rot and may harbor pests and diseases.

More Ways to Create Microclimates

WATER-FILLED PLASTIC CONTAINERS

Repurposing plastic milk containers is another way to create a thermal mass. The water-filled bottles trap heat energy from the sun during the day, which is emitted at night. These bottles can surround plants inside cold frames, greenhouses, under row covers, and out in the garden to provide supplemental heat to new plantings to assist in initial growth. Do not use glass bottles as they can break if the water freezes.

STRAW BALES

Straw bales are versatile and inexpensive and make great insulators due to the air pockets within them that retain heat, making good thermal barriers. Some gardeners in cold climates place the bales around cold frames for added protection. They can be used as windbreaks to shield transplants from extreme weather. Straw may also be applied as mulch and will break down to provide nutrients to the soil.

PLASTIC SHEETING

Plastic sheeting acts as mulch and can warm the soil a few degrees depending on the type and color used. Placing plastic sheets on the soil surface can block weed seeds from germinating. While clear plastic can raise the temperature higher than dark plastic, it encourages weed seeds to sprout as they are exposed to sunlight.

VERTICAL GARDENING

Gardening vertically is a great way to make use of microclimates. If you have a garden tower, try placing it next to or in front of a concrete, brick, or stone wall where thermal mass is captured in the daytime. Station the tower facing south or southwest for maximum light exposure.

Plant small-sized plants such as lettuces and other leafy greens as well as strawberries, radish, beets, and herbs. The middle section can be reserved for medium-sized plants such as peppers or eggplants, and the bottom can be planted with vining and larger crops such as squash and tomatoes. Or cultivate larger crops by leaving an unplanted spot to allow room for growth and air circulation.

Gardening vertically allows good airflow between plants and is less likely to shelter insect pests; therefore, plants are less prone to damage and diseases.

In addition to trellises and grow towers, fence planters are another way of gardening vertically while making efficient use of space and sheltering crops from elements.

EASY DIY TRELLIS

- 12.5- to 14-gauge welded wire fence or steel wire remesh sheet, cut to 64-inch (163-cm) length
- Two 1" x 1" x 6' (2.5 cm x 2.5 cm x 1.8 m) garden stakes
- Bolt cutters
- Staple gun or zip-ties

1. Once the site is selected, position the edge of one side of the wire fence onto a garden stake. Line up wire fence to the top of the stake, leaving 8 inches (20 cm) at the pointed side or bottom.
2. Staple or use zip-ties to secure wire onto stake. Repeat on the other side.
3. Drive the bottom of the stakes into the ground.

A garden tower is an excellent space saver while allowing you to grow numerous crops.

Companion planting allows vining cucumbers or pole beans to climb up the trellis while shading leafy greens such as lettuce and chard below.

A trellis is another great option for growing upright while maximizing space and planting in areas that aren't normally used.

SIMPLE A-FRAME TRELLIS

Cattle panels are a square grid-type fencing made of welded galvanized steel. The squares are large enough for a person's hand to fit through making it easy to reach across when harvesting. You can construct an A-frame trellis using this panel and grow shade-tolerant plants below. Plant cool-weather crops in early spring, followed by summer vining plants such as summer squash, cucumbers, or pole beans in mid- to late spring.

EASY A-FRAME TRELLIS

- Cattle panel
- Zip ties or 12.5- to 14-gauge galvanized steel wire
- Bolt cutter or hacksaw

1. Cattle panels are sold in 10-foot lengths with a height of 5 feet (1.5 m). Using a hacksaw or a bolt cutter, cut panel to desired size. Cut panels in half by cutting at the bottom of the row of squares. This will leave one of the panels with one side cut smooth and the second panel with the pointy metal rods, which are pushed into the ground when stationed.
2. Cut the horizontal wires from one end of the other panel to match up with the other panel, so both have wire rods at the bottom.
3. Line up the smooth ends of both panels and secure with a zip ties or galvanized steel wire; you will need a pair of plyers to attach these. This is the top of the trellis.
4. On one side of the garden, push the spikey end down into the soil, open the trellis to width desired. Push down the rods while stabilizing the structure.

Bamboo stakes are strong, lightweight, and inexpensive. They withstand the elements and last for years. You can easily tie three or more bamboo stakes together with twine and turn it into a teepee trellis.

PLANT HARDINESS

Plant hardiness is the ability to survive adverse growing conditions such as various climatic adversities and outdoor elements that include changes in weather, i.e., rain, wind, and snow. Certain plants can tolerate cold climates while others withstand heat and drought. Through adaptation, some plants can thrive in particular environments or atmospheric fluctuations.

The spring and fall garden should consist of cool-weather crops while heat-loving plants are grown in summer. When choosing perennial crops, acquire ones that are hardy in your climate for the best results. Refer to the chart on this page and the chart on page 52 for lists of cold-hardy crops and herbs.

SEMI- AND COLD-HARDY CROPS

Winter-kill temperature of foliage

NAME	TEMPERATURE HARDINESS
Arugula	15°F–22°F (-9.4°C to -5.5°C)
Beet	15°F–20°F (-9.4°C to -6.6°C)
Bok Choy	32°F (0°C)
Broccoli	28°F (-2.2°C)
Cabbage	25°F (-3.9°C)
Carrot	15°F (-9.4°C)
Cauliflower	32°F (0°C)
Chard	15°F–20°F (-9.4°C to -6.6°C)
Chicory	25°F (-3.9°C)
Cilantro	25°F (-3.9°C)
Claytonia	-10°F (-23°C) (-30°F, or -34°C, inside a cold frame)
Collards	0°F–10°F (-18°C to -12°C)
Curly Parsley	20 °F (-6.6 °C)
Egyptian Walking Onion	24°F (-4.4°C)
Endive	25°F (-3.9°C)
Fennel	25°F (-3.9°C)
Kale Vates Kale	10°F–15°F (-12°C to -9.4°C) 0°F (-18°C)
Jerusalem Artichoke	25°F (-3.9°C)
Leek	20°F (-7°C)
Lettuces	10°F–20°F (-12°C to -6.6°C)
Mache	0°F (-18°C)
Mizuna	25°F (-3.9°C)
Parsnip	0°F (-18°C)
Purple Sprouting Broccoli	15°F (-9.4°C)
Rhubarb	22°F (-5.5°C)
Scallions	25°F (-3.9°C)
Sorrel	32°F (0°C)
Spinach	20°F (-6.6°C)
Tatsoi	18°F–20°F (-7.7°C to -6.6°C)
Turnip	10°F–15°F (-12°C to -9.4°C)
Watercress	5°F (-15°C)

SEMI- AND COLD-HARDY HERBS

Most if not all foliage will die back in winter, but the roots of perennial plants survive the temperatures listed so they'll regenerate in spring.

Temperature hardiness for perennials

NAME	TEMPERATURE HARDINESS
Agastache (Hyssop)	-15°F (-26°C)
Bee Balm	-20°F (-29°C)
Blue Vervain	-25°F (-32°C)
Catnip	-25°F (-32°C)
Chervil	25°F (-3.9°C)
Chives	-35°F (-37°C)
Cilantro (annual)	15°F (-9.4°C)
Dill (annual)	25°F (-32°C)
Echinacea	-20°F (-28.9°C)
English Lavender	-20°F (-28.9°C)
Feverfew	-20°F (-28.9°C)
Lemon Balm	-20° F (-28.9°C)
Lovage	-15°F (-26°C)
Mint	-30° F (-34°C)
Oregano	-20°F (-28°C)
Common Self-Heal, *Prunella vulgaris*	-25°F (-32°C)
Sage	-20°F (-28°C)
Sweet Cicely (Sweet Chervil)	-25°F (-32°C)
Tansy	-40°F (-40°C)
Tarragon	-35°F (-37°C)
Thyme	-20°F (-28.9°C)
Wild Fennel	-35°F (-37°C)

HEAT-TOLERANT CROPS

- Amaranth
- Chard
- Collards
- Corn
- Cucumber
- Eggplant
- Kale
- Lettuce ('Black Seeded Simpson', 'Parris Island')
- Luffa Gourd
- Malabar Spinach
- Melon
- Mizuna and 'Red Giant' Mustard
- Okra
- Peppers (Sweet and Hot)
- Summer Squash (Zucchini)
- Sweet Potato
- Tomato
- Yard-Long Beans

PLANTS THAT THRIVE IN PART-SUN

Plants grown in part-sun (3–6 hours/day) will mature at a slower rate compared to crops planted in full sun.

- Arugula
- Bok Choy
- Broccoli
- Brussels Sprouts
- Bunching Onion (Scallion)
- Cauliflower
- Chard
- Chives (tolerates part-shade in warm climates)
- Celery
- Collards
- Egyptian Walking Onion
- Garden Cress
- Horseradish
- Kale
- Leek
- Lettuce
- Mizuna
- Mustard Greens
- Napa Cabbage
- Potato
- Rhubarb
- Spinach

SHADE-TOLERANT HERBS

- Bay Laurel
- Chervil
- Chives
- Cilantro
- Corsican Mint
- Garlic Chives
- Lemon Balm
- Lemon Verbena
- Lovage
- Marjoram
- Mint
- Oregano
- Parsley (Flat-leaf and Curly)
- Sorrel
- Sweet Cicely (Sweet Chervil)
- Tarragon

SEASON EXTENDERS

You put in time and hard work planting cool-season crops, now it's time to do what you can to lengthen your growing season. There are several ways to prolong harvests and speed germination as well as establish transplants quicker. This can be accomplished by maintaining microclimates to retain sufficient heat while keeping the cold and other harsh conditions out. The following techniques are useful in spring and into fall through winter to extend the harvest of cold-hardy crops such as those listed in the chart on page 51.

Row Covers

Since we live in a mild region, I generally use horticultural fleece draped over and attached to hoop structures. It's a lightweight non-woven polypropylene material that's essentially fabric that allows up to 70 percent sunlight transmission as well as allowing precipitation and overhead irrigation to pass through. Additionally, the material helps retain heat and moisture. You may consider a heavier weight especially if you live in a colder area. Thicker fabric will decrease sunlight penetration, although plants are usually dormant through cold winters and can tolerate a few days without much light. If you receive an abundance of snow, don't let it pile up as it will cause your structures to collapse and extended periods without daylight may be fatal to crops. In anticipation of snow, place plastic sheeting over the low tunnel to allow snow to slide down.

Horticultural fleece may also give young seedlings that are planted in late winter or early spring a head start while providing shelter from the elements. It's also a good windbreak. Some gardeners use plastic covers; however, those require venting, especially on mild days as the temperature inside can rise rapidly when outdoor temperatures exceed 50°F (10°C). In colder climates, this is a benefit and can offer more protection when placed over another barrier. Row covers may be utilized inside high tunnels as well as in an unheated greenhouse. Furthermore, a garden cover can be used to shade crops from scorching sun in summer and act as a barrier from insect or animal pests. Other ways to shelter your crops during winter are to place a cold frame over a raised bed or to build one that is partially in the ground for added insulation. Cold frame and greenhouse kits including portable types are offered in various designs and prices. You may also construct a high or low tunnel hoop house or utilize an unheated greenhouse to shield winter-hardy crops.

A collapsible polydome is easily placed on rows of crops and retracts for easy storage.

Greenhouse kits with polycarbonate panels have excellent light transmission as well as heat retention.

Greenhouse construction with plastic or greenhouse film such as polyethylene is an economical option.

Low Tunnels

A low tunnel or hoop house can be set up using store-bought wire hoops, which come in different dimensions. A row cover is attached to the hoops with garden clips, although clothespins or binder clips work too. Secure the sides and ends to prevent the cover from blowing away. You may use rocks or wood boards to keep the fabric in place, being careful not to snag or tear the material. With proper use and care, horticultural fleece and plastic can last a few years. Constructing a low tunnel using PVC pipes is another option.

SIMPLE LOW TUNNEL

This is for a bed measuring 6 x 3 feet (1.8 x 0.9 m). For longer beds you will need an additional PVC pipe and 2 rebar stakes for every 2 feet (60 cm) of length. The hoops are spaced 2 feet (60 cm) apart.

- 3 10-foot (3-m) PVC pipes of ½-inch (1-cm) diameter
- 6 rebar stakes (18-inch or 45-cm lengths)
- Garden fleece or plastic

1. Use a rubber mallet to push the rebar stakes to a depth of 8–10 inches (20–25.5 cm) leaving about 8–10 inches (20–25.5 cm) aboveground. Stakes should be placed in all four corners of the bed and two between.
2. Fit one end of the pipe over the rebar making a hoop to place over the rebar on the opposite side and repeat.
3. Drape the garden fleece or plastic and fasten with clips or clamps. Cut excess fabric and secure ends with scrap wood, large rocks, or bricks. If you are using a plastic sheeting, make sure to vent your low tunnel on days when temperature is above 50° F (10°C) to prevent overheating.

Cold Frames

A bottomless cold frame can be like an unheated greenhouse. The structure has a clear lid to allow soil to absorb and store thermal mass from the sunlight during the day and release it as heat at nighttime. Select a level location that drains well. The transparent lid of the cold frame will have a slanted side; this should face south or southeast for maximum daylight exposure. The instructions below are for a wooden frame with polycarbonate panel lid. Other designs make use of refurbished windows or shower doors. Structures that can be used to build cold frames include straw bales, concrete blocks, or bricks. In winter, place a heavy blanket over the structure on cold nights to help retain heat generated during the day. The inside of a cold frame can maintain temperatures a few degrees warmer than its surroundings. Cold frames should be vented (cracked open) when daytime temperatures rise above 50°F (10°C) to prevent overheating; close them in the evening.

HOW TO MAKE A COLD FRAME

This cold frame measures 6 x 3 feet (1.8 x 0.9 m) with a 12-inch (30-cm) depth angled upward to an 18-inch (45-cm) slope (which should face south or southeast). We used 2 boards at the front, 3 at the back, and 5 shorter boards to enclose the sides. The fifth shorter board is cut in half diagonally to match the slope.

- Twin wall polycarbonate panel cut to size and secured to a wooden frame
- Pressure-treated lumber
- 8 cedar boards (1 inch x 6 inches x 6 feet, or 2.5 cm x 15 cm x 1.8 m)
- 4 corner posts cut to match height of frame
- 4 hinges
- Screws
- Drill
- Screwdriver
- Frame

1. Cut three of the boards in half, each measuring 3 feet (90 cm) in length. Five of these will be your side boards with one cut in half diagonally. You'll have two of the same triangular-shaped boards, which should match the slope.
2. Save the sixth 3-foot (90-cm) board to support the lid when it needs to be opened.
3. Measure and cut vertical posts to the height of the front and back of the frame.
4. Attach side boards onto posts securing with two screws at each end of the boards. The top triangular boards should be attached vertically at both sides with the narrow end screwed into the board beneath.
5. Attach the front and back boards to the corner posts the same way.
6. Place the lid on the frame ensuring it's flush with the back side. Place and screw on the hinges spaced apart equally.
7. Vent your cold frame on mild days as temperatures inside can rise quickly. Use the extra board for propping up the lid.

Starting Seeds Indoors

Starting crops from seed prolongs the seasons and comes with numerous benefits. It saves money and presents more options than what Big Box stores and nurseries offer. It's a great skill to learn, and you'll witness the growing stages of various plants from seeding to harvest, which is exciting and rewarding! When selecting varieties, pick plants that are suitable for your climate and ones that your family likes and will eat. Choosing the right crops for each season as well as those that perform well in your region leads to great results. For example, we tend to grow tomato varieties that don't require a long season due to our mild and cool weather. We've had success cultivating short-season or early-maturing varieties. For the majority of crops, start seeds indoors 6-8 weeks before your last spring frost. If you start too early, you may have to transplant more than once and house them inside for longer periods until outdoor conditions are favorable. Certain seeds such as rosemary and thyme are slow to germinate and can take 2–4 weeks to sprout. Start these earlier so they're ready to plant after the likelihood of frost has passed.

GROW LIGHTS

Before you start seeds indoors, select a well-ventilated area. If the room has poor ventilation, add a fan to provide air circulation as lack of air exposure can lead to mold and a fungal disease known as damping off. For grow lights, you can find inexpensive shop lights such as fluorescent tube lamps at most hardware stores. When selecting lamps, look for the color temperature on the packaging followed by the letter "K" (for Kelvin).

For example, a 5,000–6,500K lamp will provide the light spectrum necessary for foliage growth; this is considered a cool light. Warm light indicates a lower color temperature. Most stores offer LED lights, which are more energy efficient although they cost more. LED bulbs generally have a longer life, and you'll save on your energy bills since they're more efficient.

HOW TO START SEEDS INDOORS

1. Obtain planting cells, trays, and pots; you can also repurpose yogurt cups and other plastic containers. The pots must be 2–3 inches (5–7.5 cm) deep with drainage holes at the bottom. I use pots with a 3-inch (7.5-cm) diameter as this provides plenty of room for a seedling to grow until I plant them outdoors.
2. Buy a seed-starter mix for your potting medium or make your own. Potting mix must be sterile and lightweight. Avoid substituting garden soil as it's too heavy for seedlings to push through and may introduce pathogens. I usually add 1 part worm castings to my seed-starter mix to feed seedlings. Prepare your potting soil by adding water to moisten but not saturate. For instructions on making your own seed-starter and potting mixes, see page 87.
3. Fill the pots with the dampened mix and press firmly. Plant seeds according to the directions on their seed packet. You may use a dibbler or a pencil to make shallow depressions to bury seeds. Seed depth should be about twice the width of the seed. Avoid burying tiny seeds deeply. Sow 2–3 seeds per pot; not all seeds will sprout. If they all germinate, snip all but the healthiest one or you can separate the seedlings if you wish.

   Some seeds such as lettuce and celery require exposure to light to break dormancy and germinate. Barely cover them with moist soil or lightly sprinkle about ⅛ inch (3 mm) of soil over them.
4. After sowing, moisten the seeds by misting or use a small watering can with a rose fitting. Gently water seeds in to avoid dislodging from soil. Place plastic wrap or a plastic dome over the pots or trays to maintain humidity; this will keep soil and seeds moist. When you see signs of germination, remove humidity dome and place the pots under grow lights. The distance can be as close as 2–4 inches (5–10 cm) unless your light runs hot; then you'll need to place them farther away. Test the heat dissipated from the light by placing the back of your hand beneath at a distance where it feels comfortable. This is where the top of your seedlings should be. It's essential that seedlings receive adequate lighting to grow strong and healthy stems; if they're too far away, they'll stretch toward the light source resulting in leggy and weak seedlings. Many light fixtures hang from chains and their height can be adjusted. You may also stack books or wood blocks to bring seedlings closer to the light. Lights can be left on at least 12–16 hours per day; set a timer for convenience. As seedlings grow, raise the light or remove the blocks.
5. Keep seedlings watered and fed. Lightly water from the top but avoid wetting the foliage, or water from the bottom by placing the pots in a water-filled tray. Let them sit in the tray for a few minutes as the soil takes up moisture through capillary action. Remove the pots from the water when the top of the soil is moist; the pots will feel heavier. Don't saturate as it can block oxygen and may lead to root rot. Liquid fertilizer can be diluted in water to feed the seedlings regularly. Follow the directions and recommendations on the label.

HARDENING-OFF SEEDLINGS

Acclimating plants to the outdoors is necessary before transplanting; this is referred to as "hardening-off" and usually takes about 7 days. Your little seedlings have been pampered and nurtured indoors in a controlled environment and need to be introduced gradually to the outdoors. Skipping this process and planting seedlings directly outside can shock them and may even be fatal. Ensure that the soil is evenly moist during the transition. On the first day, place your seedlings in a sheltered area for one hour, away from direct sunlight and protected from strong winds and rain. Set your seedlings on a tray to make it easier to move them outside and back into the house. When you bring them indoors, place them back under grow lights for the remainder of each day. As the seedlings are placed outdoors add one hour per day for 7 days. By the seventh day, your plants should be ready to plant in your garden.

By now you might have already decided the location of your edible landscape. Remember to create a healthy foundation so your plants will thrive and perform well. In this chapter I introduced you to various techniques and structures such as using mulches, constructing mini hoop houses, and building cold frames to mitigate weather changes and to extend your harvests. Some of these are applied throughout the season and may also serve as multi-purpose methods. The next chapters will go over season-by-season tasks, maintenance, tips, and DIY projects, as well as lists of crops to plant in succession and harvest within each season. You will also find information for incorporating and planting perennial vegetables, herbs, and fruiting shrubs and trees that will generate nutritious and delicious produce for years to come.

4
SPRING

In spring, you may notice the chorus of birds becomes more prominent. Rainy days invite them to feast on earthworms from thawed ground while small mammals forage in the garden. Longer days and increasing daylight warm the soil, awakening plants from hibernation. The buds arousing from winter dormancy on berry shrubs, canes, and fruit trees start to form. Prune berry canes as soon as possible. When conditions outside are favorable, you may start acclimating indoor seed starts to plant out in the garden. For instructions on acclimating plants, see page 59.

Refer to the sidebar on page 51 for a complete list of crops that perform well in cool spring temperatures. It's best to harvest these vegetables before warm weather makes them go to seed. "Bolting" crops develop a bitter flavor and are not palatable. Overwintered root crops must be harvested by early spring, before they set flowers, as roots tend to become pithy and tough.

This is also a good time to plan and implement crop rotation and to plant crops that performed well in the prior season. In this chapter I'll go over certain techniques for a productive spring garden, which include maximizing space, increasing yields, and extending your harvests.

Fall-planted crops that wintered over are harvested early in the season. Some that we grow year-round include kale, collards, mizuna, tatsoi, spinach (shown above), mache, claytonia, and bunching onions.

HARVEST NOW

Spring Vegetables: Overwintered Vegetables Under Cover

- Arugula
- Beet
- Brussels Sprouts
- Cabbage
- Carrot
- Chard
- Claytonia
- Collards
- Garlic Greens
- Kale
- Leek
- Lettuce
- Mache
- Mustard Greens
- Purple Sprouting Broccoli
- Scallion
- Sorrel
- Spinach
- Tatsoi

Spring Herbs

This list consists of some that overwinter and some that are starting to emerge.

- Chives
- Cilantro (self-seeded)
- Lavender
- Lemon Balm
- Marjoram
- Mint
- Oregano*
- Parsley
- Rosemary*
- Sage*
- Sweet Cicely (Sweet Chervil)
- Winter Savory*
- Tarragon
- Thyme*
- Wild Fennel

**Overwintered*

Leeks are an easy crop to overwinter and can be harvested anytime from fall through the following spring.

Evergreen perennial herbs such as rosemary, bay leaf, sage, oregano, thyme, winter savory, and mint are also available to harvest. Some deciduous varieties of perennial herbs require time to regenerate as they lose their foliage in the cold months.

WHAT TO PLANT NOW

If you started seeds indoors, be sure to acclimate them. Check out your local nursery or garden center for seedlings and young plants if you didn't start any indoors.

Transplant Now: Early to Late Spring

- Brassicas (Broccoli, Cauliflower, Cabbage, Collards, Kale)
- Herbs
- Leafy Greens (Lettuces, Spinach, Chard)
- Leek
- Onion
- Shallots

Crops to Sow Under Cover

Why wait till the last spring frost when you can plant now using season extenders? Several cool-season crops can be sowed a few weeks before your last frost date. Some will even germinate in soil temperatures as low as 40°F (4.4°C). The microclimate inside a hoop house, cold frame, or greenhouse can give you a couple of weeks' head-start to a spring garden and earlier harvests! A row cover will act as a barrier to protect vegetables from light spring frosts. Another technique you may want to try is winter sowing, outlined in chapter 7.

- Beet
- Broccoli
- Carrot
- Cauliflower
- Chard
- Collard
- Kale

Plastic or glass choches placed over spring transplants provide an extra layer of protection from spring frosts.

Arugula is one of the earliest crops you can plant in your spring garden.

Lettuce seeds are best sown on the surface as they benefit from being exposed to sunlight, which breaks dormancy.

Direct Sow, No Cover

These can be planted in early spring as soon as the soil is workable.

- Arugula
- Asparagus crowns
- Bok Choy
- Borage
- Chives
- Cilantro
- Claytonia
- Dill
- Jerusalem Artichoke
- Lemon Balm (keep contained, invasive)
- Lettuce
- Mache
- Oca tubers
- Onion sets
- Orach
- Parsley
- Peas
- Potato
- Radish
- Rhubarb crowns
- Spinach
- Tatsoi
- Yacon tubers

TOP 10 FAST-GROWING SPRING VEGETABLES

BABY GREENS IN 30 DAYS OR LESS	DAYS TO MATURITY
Arugula	45
Bok Choy	45 (extra-dwarf variety matures in 30 days)
Chard	50-60
Collards	75
Kale	55-75
Leaf Lettuce	45-55
Mustard Greens	30-60
Radish	21-35
Spinach	45
Tatsoi	45 (dwarf variety matures in 25 days)

Direct Sow or Transplant

These can be sown from mid to late spring after the soil has warmed and the danger of frost has passed.

- Bean
- Corn
- Cucumber
- Eggplant
- Melon
- Okra
- Pepper
- Pumpkin
- Sweet Potato Slips
- Summer Squash
- Tomato
- Winter Squash

Try planting several varieties of the same crop with differing maturity dates. For example, most leaf lettuce fully develops in 45–55 days while heading varieties such as Romaine take 75–85 days and crisphead takes 70–100 days. Plant radishes between leafy greens, onions, or garlic; they'll mature in about 3–4 weeks. By the time the radishes are harvested, your other crops will have sufficient time to develop and mature.

SPRING TIPS AND TASKS

AMEND GARDEN BEDS AND TURN COVER CROPS

If you applied a layer of compost to your beds in fall, you may plant in it directly. However, if you are just now adding compost, let it settle about two weeks before planting. The microbes and other soil organisms will break it down further allowing nutrients to be bioavailable for plants to uptake. Tilling is not necessary. Earthworms and other soil organisms feed on organic matter and burrow—over time, compost is incorporated into the soil. Turn under cover crops planted in late summer or fall when the ground isn't too wet in spring. Allow the vegetation and roots to decompose 3–4 weeks before planting. Cover crops are discussed in chapter 6.

SPRING TIPS AND TASKS

UNDERSTANDING TYPES OF PLANTS

You may notice plant tags are usually marked "Annual, Biennial, or Perennial." Most cultivated vegetable crops are annuals and biennials. Annuals complete their life cycle in one growing season and die back. They develop vegetative growth, flower, and produce seeds all in one season. Annual plants are planted yearly.

Biennials have a two-year life cycle, growing roots, stems, and foliage in their first year. During the second season biennials "bolt" (flower) and then produce seeds and die. Several biennial crops are normally grown as annuals including carrots, beets, chard, kale, celery, and parsley.

Perennials live three years or longer. Their roots remain in the ground and don't die back, regenerating for consecutive seasons. Evergreen types retain leaves year-round while herbaceous varieties die back in winter. When choosing a perennial, make sure it's hardy to your climate. Like annuals and biennials, perennials can be propagated from seeds. Berries, fruit trees, and herbs are great perennials to integrate into an edible landscape.

GROWING FRUITS AND BERRIES

We enjoy growing several types of fruiting canes, shrubs, and fruit trees. Once they're established and properly maintained, they'll yield bountiful harvests of delightful garden treats for many years! Certain berry and fruit trees require cross-pollination to set fruit. Cross-pollination can improve fruit quality, size, and flavor while maintaining genetic diversity. Select varieties that are hardy in your climate to ensure well-performing cultivars. Vernalization (a period of chill hours) is necessary for flower and fruit set in several berry and fruit variants. Calculate the number of days or hours that fall below 40°F (4.4°C) in your climate to determine which variety will excel. Obtain dormant strawberry crowns, berry shrubs, canes, and fruit trees. Plant them as soon as you have them on hand in prepared holes, containers, or beds.

RASPBERRY

- Raspberry, *Rubus idaeus*, is a member of the rose family, *Rosaceae*.
- Raspberries come in summer-bearing and everbearing types.
- Everbearing raspberries produce once more the following summer on the same canes, which become floricanes or second-year canes. Standard raspberries usually require 800+ chill hours below 45°F (7°C).

ADVANTAGES OF BARE-ROOT PLANTS

Not only are bare-root plants less expensive, they're also not growing in a pot of soil, which makes them much easier to manage. It's simpler to inspect the roots for potential damage and they can be trimmed more easily. The roots are usually not rootbound, which can occur in some potted plants. Bare-root plants transition well and develop faster as they don't have to adapt to a new soil environment like potted plants do.

Bare-root plants are usually packed in moist wood shavings or sawdust. They should be planted before they break dormancy and as soon as the ground is workable in late winter or early spring. Most of our fruit trees and berries were started from bare-root plants.

Summer-bearing raspberry will set fruit on second-year or fruiting canes called "floricanes." Prune old canes that have already produced fruit down to the ground each spring.

HOW TO PLANT RASPBERRIES

Select a sunny area that receives 6 hours of sunlight or more and remove any weeds. Raspberries thrive in part-shade but won't be as fruitful. Plant in well-drained soil rich in organic matter; excessive soil moisture can lead to root rot. Raspberries will grow in sandy loam as long as it's fertile. Plant in prepared beds or till in finished compost 6–12 inches (15–30 cm) deep. The upright canes require support; provide a trellis. Some dwarf cultivars are available that don't need trellising and can be grown in large containers.

1. Soak dormant bare-root canes for an hour or two before planting.
2. Rows should be 1–2 feet (30–60 cm) wide. If planting more than one row, space each row 6–8 feet (1.8–2.4 m) apart. Raspberries can be grown in framed beds, but you may have to dedicate the entire bed to this crop as it can take over most of the space.
3. Dig a trench through the center of each row.
4. Space 18–24 inches (45–60 cm) apart.
5. Cover and press soil around the roots with the upper roots about ½ inch (1.3 cm) beneath the soil surface.
6. Water after planting and 1–2 inches (2.5–5 cm) weekly during the growing season.

Each raspberry plant can yield 1–2 quarts (0.9–1.9 L).

It's important to maintain your raspberry bed by removing new canes (primocanes) that emerge in between rows or outside of the bed.

Some blueberries are self-fertile, although planting two or more cultivars is beneficial. Cross-pollination can increase berry quality and size.

BLUEBERRY

Blueberry, *Vaccinium*, is related to azaleas and rhododendrons and is a member of the heather family, *Ericaceae*. Blueberry shrubs require a certain number of chill hours (vernalization) to regenerate and set fruit. Select cultivars that are acclimated to your area. Depending on the variety, the number of chill hours can range from 200–1,000+.

TYPES OF BLUEBERRIES

Northern Highbush: Highbush blueberries, *Vaccinium corymbosum*, are native to the eastern and northeastern United States. These shrubs can grow 5–9 feet tall and are typically cold-hardy to -20°F to -30°F (-29°C to -34°C).

Lowbush: Lowbush, *Vaccinium angustifolium*, are adapted to colder climates and hardy to about -40°F (-40°C). Lowbush blueberries are native to the northeastern United States, Virginia, Minnesota, and the eastern region of Canada (Maritime Provinces). These low-growing shrubs have a height usually no more than 24 inches (60 cm).

Rabbiteye: Rabbiteye types, *Vaccinium virgatum*, are native to the southeastern United States. These cultivars are suitable for regions with long, hot summers and are hardy to around 5°F–0°F (-15°C to -18°C). They grow to 6–10 feet (1.8–3 m), sometimes taller if they're not maintained.

Hybrid Half-high: Half-high blueberries are developed by crossing northern highbush and lowbush types. Half-high cultivars grow 3–4 feet (0.9–1.2 m) tall and are very cold hardy to -35°F–45°F (1.7°C–7.2°C).

Southern Highbush: Southern highbush are hybrids of *V. corymbosum*, *V. virgatum*, and *V. darrowii*.

These cultivars were developed for regions with mild winters and require fewer chill hours, typically around 200–300.

HOW TO PLANT A BLUEBERRY

Blueberries thrive in acidic soil with a pH of 4.5–5.5. It's a good idea to test your native soil before planting as soil with a high pH will slow growth and cause poor fruit production. If the soil is alkaline, nutrients get locked up, making them inaccessible for plants. However, there are cultivars that grow well in containers, which gives you control over the soil. You may use prepared soil mixes such as ones for azaleas and camellias, which usually run acidic. Combine equal parts soil mix and shredded bark or coconut peat. This allows the soil to drain well and promotes healthy root growth. Select a container at least 18–20 inches (45–50 cm) in diameter and make sure it has drainage holes. For planting in raised beds, mix equal parts peat moss and a raised bed mix. Peat moss is acidic with a pH of 4.4.

1. Select 2- to 3-year-old dormant plants in early spring and remove any damaged canes, roots, or diseased parts.
2. Choose a sunny location with loose, well-drained, fertile soil. Prepare the bed and till in compost to 6 inches (15 cm) deep. Add the recommend amount of elemental sulfur as necessary based on a soil test. This can be mixed into soil a few months prior to planting.
3. Remove any weeds as they'll compete for water and nutrients.
4. Space 4–5 feet (1.2–1.5 m) apart or 2½–3 feet (70–90 cm) apart if you're growing blueberries as hedgerows. Space rows 8 feet (2.4 m) apart.
5. Dig a hole twice the width and depth of the plant's roots.
6. Set the rootball into the planting hole no more than ½ inch (1 cm) below the surface.
7. Backfill; pack firmly.
8. Water after planting and mulch a 2- to 3-inch (5- to 7.5-cm) layer of wood chips, peat moss, pine needles, shredded bark, or sawdust. Keep mulch at least 4 inches (10 cm) away from the stems to prevent disease or insect infestations.

Allow blueberry plants to establish and promote vegetative growth by pinching off the blossoms. Remove all flowers in the first year and leave about 30 percent in the second. This will create strong and vigorous plants resulting in better yields in following years.

Gooseberry shrub

Currants

Himalayan honeysuckle

OTHER FRUIT SHRUBS TO CONSIDER

Gooseberry and currants are very cold-hardy and require a certain number of chill hours (vernalization) depending on the variety. They can be planted in 15-gallon (19-L) pots with an 18-inch (45-cm) diameter. Both are shade-tolerant and can be situated under fruit or nut trees.

Gooseberry (*Ribes uva-crispa*, Currant family, Grossulariaceae): Gooseberry is typically hardy to -40°F (-40°C) and requires 1,000–1,200 chill hours. The canes can grow 3–10 feet (0.9–3 m) tall. The berries taste like tangy grapes.

Currant (*Ribes*, Currant family, Grossulariaceae): While most currants are hardy to -40°F (-40°C), Alpine currant is hardy down to -50°F (-45.5°C). Currants need 1,200–2,500 chill hours and will grow 3–6 feet (0.9–1.8 m) tall and wide. Their small jewel-like berries have a sour-and-sweet taste with just the right balance.

Himalayan Honeysuckle (*Leycesteria formosa*, Honeysuckle family, Caprifoliaceae): This Himalayan native can be grown both in warm and cool climates; it's a semi-hardy perennial shrub to 0°F (-17.8°C). Due to its potentially invasive nature, consider planting it in a large container (15 to 20 gallons, or 57 to 76 L). The berries have a distinct flavor between burnt caramel and toffee; some describe the taste as being like coffee and raisins.

STRAWBERRY

The garden strawberry (*Fragaria* x *ananassa*) is a member of the rose family, Rosaceae. Strawberries are a wonderful perennial crop for home gardens as they're fun to grow and can be planted in several ways including in-ground, framed beds, and containers. They can be situated in small spaces such as vertical garden towers, hanging baskets, fabric grow bags, or window box planters. They look great in terracotta pots! Strawberries make a nice edible groundcover or edging plant. There are three types of strawberries to consider and numerous varieties to select from.

POPULAR STRAWBERRY VARIETIES

Select cultivars adapted to your growing region for the best results.

- June Bearing: 'Earliglow', 'Allstar', 'Jewel', 'Chandler', 'Sparkle'
- Everbearing: 'Quinault', 'Ozark Beauty', 'Fort Laramie'
- Day Neutral: 'Tristar', 'Seascape', 'Albion', 'San Andreas'

Strawberries have shallow root systems. A container with a diameter of 10–12 inches (25.5–30 cm) and a depth of 8 inches (20 cm) should be adequate for one strawberry plant, although it's not a bad idea to go with a larger pot so you don't have to water as often. Replenish the potting soil yearly in winter or early spring.

TYPES OF STRAWBERRIES

June Bearing: June-bearing strawberry plants typically produce one crop for 2–3 weeks in spring and early summer. The flowerbuds blossom in spring and produce large berries between June and July. June-bearers are vigorous and produce a dense mat of runners.

Everbearing: This type produces two large crops, once in early summer and again in fall with very few berries in between. Everbearing varieties do not produce many runners.

Day-Neutral: Day neutral types generally produce throughout the growing season and develop few runners.

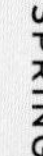

Strawberries are a great candidate for grow towers. Plant one crown in each segment. Rotate the tower 180 degrees daily so the plants receive sufficient sunlight.

HOW TO PLANT BARE-ROOT STRAWBERRIES

Bare-root strawberries are bundles of dormant crowns with roots that are much easier to plant than live potted plants. Bundles are generally sold with 25 crowns, but smaller bundles are available. Planting sites should receive full sun with sandy loam or any well-drained soil rich in organic matter. Plant crowns in late winter or early spring after the danger of frost has passed.

1. Trim the roots to about 4–5 inches (10–13 cm).
2. June bearing: Space 18 inches (45 cm) apart in rows 4 feet (1.2 m) apart. Strawberries develop stolons or runners in all directions and will root easily. They will eventually form a new row in between the main rows if allowed to proliferate.
3. Everbearing and day neutral: Space 1 foot (30 cm) apart in rows 1 foot (30 cm) apart. Allow plants to establish and grow large by removing runners.
4. Plant in a trench 6 inches (15 cm) deep or in a planting hole.
5. Place the crown and spread out its roots making sure the crown is at the soil surface.
6. Cover the roots with soil and press firmly.
7. Water and apply a 1-inch (2.5-cm) layer of straw mulch around the plants.

Fig trees are a great addition to a four-season food garden.

FRUIT TREES

Most fruit trees thrive best in well-drained soil. Select cultivars that are acclimated to your region. In the Pacific Northwest, apples, pears, plums, cherries, and other stone fruits can be grown with success, but not most citrus. Since citrus trees are subtropical plants, they need warm weather and plenty of sunshine. However, there are semi-hardy cultivars such as 'Yuzu' citrus that can tolerate 0°F (-17.8°C) and 'Meyer' lemon (32°F, or 0°C). Fig is a subtropical plant requiring warm days; however, some varieties can withstand subfreezing temperatures, even as low as -20°F (-29°C). Hardy fig varieties include 'Violette de Bordeaux' (-20°F, or -29°C), 'Chicago' (-20°F, or -29°C), 'English Brown Turkey' (0°F, -17.8°C). We currently grow 'Dessert King' (5°F, -15°C) and 'Italian Honey' (10°F, or -12°C).

With grafting technology, you can obtain a tree with multiple varieties of fruit grafted onto a single tree.

If you want to grow apples, you'll need another variety to cross-pollinate it to bear fruit. That can be achieved by purchasing one tree that's been grafted with several types of apples that are compatible for cross-pollination.

We have fruit trees grafted with 3–5 different types. These make excellent alternatives especially for small areas. If you have space restrictions, choose the extra- or ultra-dwarf trees that mature to just under 6 feet (1.8 m). These smaller varieties can be grown in large containers with a diameter of 18–22 inches (46–56 cm). While mature standard fruit trees can reach a height and width of 18–25 feet (5.5–7.6 m), semi-dwarf types get to 12–18 feet (3.6–5.5 m) both in height and width. Dwarf trees grow to about 8–10 feet (2.4–3 m) (tall and wide), and ultra-dwarf tops at around 3–6 feet (0.9–1.8 m). Lastly, grow fruits that you and or your family like to eat which is, of course, the primary reason you're planting a miniature backyard orchard.

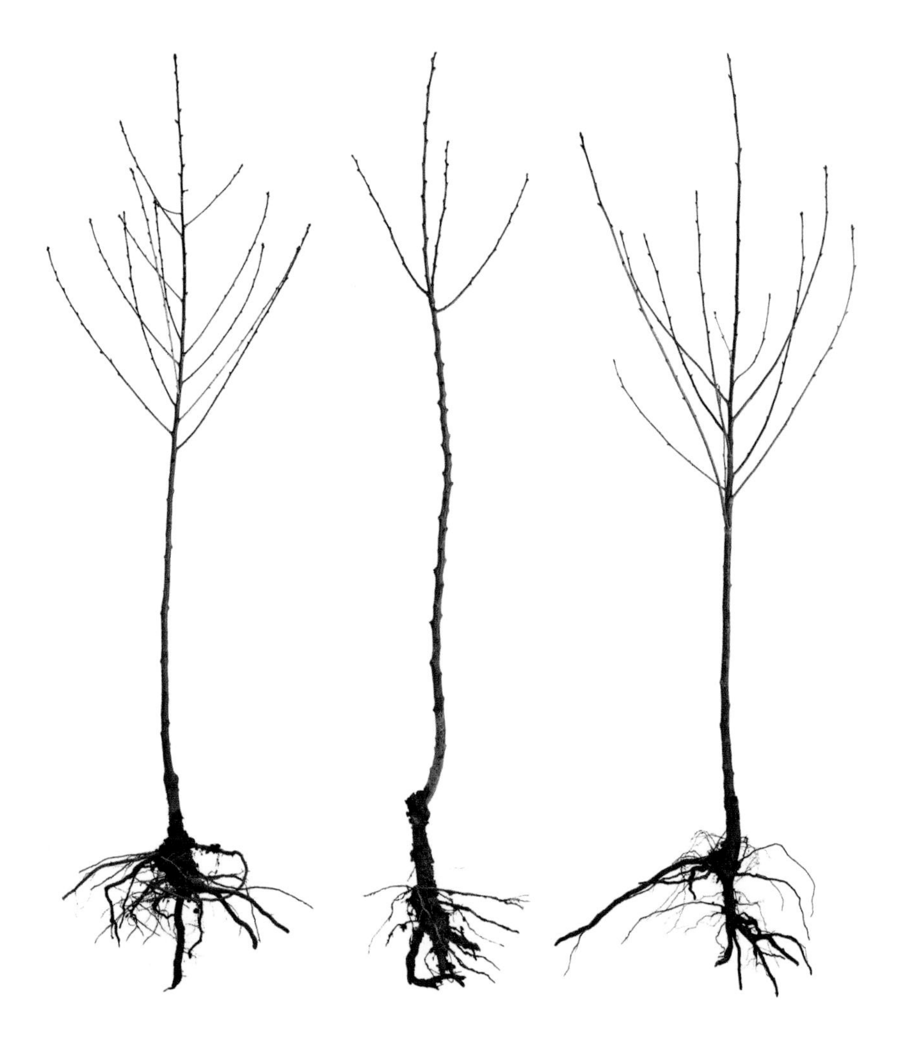

A dwarf tree is developed by joining the shoot system of a chosen cultivar, or "scion wood," to a rootstock. The rootstock determines the size of the tree. The scion will produce vegetative growth, flowers, and fruits. Sometimes the scion wood may be grafted onto an interstem, which is grafted onto the rootstock. It is essentially having two rootstocks embedded together. This image shows three bare-root grafted fruit trees ready for planting.

FRUIT TREE HEIGHT AND SPACING REQUIREMENTS

Basic requirements and results will vary depending on the cultivar and environment.

FRUIT TREE	TREE HEIGHT	SPACING
Standard Apple and Cherry Trees	18–25 feet (5.5–7.6 m)	35 x 35 feet (10.7 x 10.7 m)
Standard Fruit Trees	18–25 feet (5.5–7.6 m)	20 x 20 feet (6 x 6 m)
Semi-Dwarf	12–15 feet (3.6–4.5 m)	15 x 15 feet (4.5 x 4.5 m)
Dwarf	8–10 feet (2.4–3 m)	10 x 10 feet (3 x 3 m)
Ultra-Dwarf	3–6 feet (0.9–1.8 m)	6 feet (1.8 m) apart or in a container (18- to 22-inch [46- to 56-cm] diameter)

HOW TO PLANT A FRUIT TREE

1. Select a sunny area with well-drained soil.
2. Dig a hole 11–12 inches (28–30 cm) deep or about 2–3 inches (5–7.5 cm) more than the root's depth with a width 2–3 times the width of the roots.
3. Place a mound of soil mixed with compost at the bottom of the hole.
4. Place the tree in the center of the hole at the same level it was before. The root flare should be just above the soil level.
5. Most fruit trees are grafted onto a rootstock. The area where the scion and rootstock join should remain above the soil surface.
6. Backfill the planting hole with native soil mixed with some compost. Gently firm the soil around the tree to remove air pockets, making sure the tree is upright and straight. It's important to remove large air pockets to prevent roots from dehydrating.
7. Create a shallow basin around the tree for watering. Water in well and allow to drain and settle in.
8. Place 2–3 inches (5–7.5 cm) of organic mulch, keeping it at least 6 inches (15 cm) away from the tree trunk to prevent rot, disease, or pest damage.
9. Staking isn't necessary if a tree is planted properly. If you prefer to stake to safeguard the tree from strong winds, secure it into the planting hole right before the tree is placed. Tie the tree to the stake.

SPRING TIPS AND TASKS

PLANT PERENNIAL VEGETABLES

Perennial vegetables are wonderful additions to a four-season food garden. They provide reliable harvests for years and can be grown in out-of-the-way areas or within the garden itself. Yes, some are more unusual than others, but some perennial vegetables should be staples in every garden.

Below you will find a chart of some of my favorite perennial vegetables along with the lowest winter temperature they'll survive. For a harvest that lasts years instead of weeks, incorporate some of these tasty plants into your garden.

TYPES OF PERENNIAL VEGETABLES

PLANT NAME	ROOT HARDINESS TEMPERATURE
Asparagus	-40°F (-40°C)
Bunching Onion (Scallion)	-10°F (-23°C)
Cardoon	10°F (-12°C)
Chicory (Radicchio, short-lived perennial)	20°F
Claytonia	-10°F (-23°C)
Earth Chestnut	-10°F (-23°C)
Egyptian Walking Onion	-40°F
Globe Artichoke	10°F (-12°C)
Jerusalem Artichoke	-40°F (-40°C)
'Kaleidoscopic Kale-Grex'	10°F–15°F (-12°C to -9.3°C)
'Kosmic' Kale	10°F–15°F (-12°C to -9.3°C)
Leek	-20°F (-29°C)
Multiplier Onion (Potato Onion)	-20°F (-29°C)

PLANT NAME	ROOT HARDINESS TEMPERATURE
Nodding Onion	-30°F (-34°C)
Oca (*Oxalis tuberosa*)	15–20°F (-6.7–9.3°C)
Rhubarb	-40°F (-40°C)
Scarlet Runner Beans	10°F (-12°C)
Seakale (*Crambe maritima*)	-30°F (-34°C)
Sorrel (Herb, prepared like potherb)	-30°F (-34°C)
Sweet Cicely (edible roots, leaves, flowers, and seeds)	-20°F (-29°C)
Tree Collards	20°F–15°F (-6.7°C to -9.3°C)
Watercress (*Nasturtium officinale*)	-40°F (-40°C)
Wild Arugula (Wall Rocket, Sylvetta)	-15°F–20°F (-26°C to -6.7°C)
Yacon (Tuberous crop)	15°F (-18°C) (Protect crown with thick mulch or overwinter indoors)

CHOOSE A PLANTING METHOD

BIODIVERSITY GARDENING

Growing an assortment of plants adds biodiversity while creating an attractive feature in the garden. Biodiverse plots rebuild, maintain, and preserve ecosystems for future generations. There are several advantages to growing different crops together and incorporating ones that are pest- and disease-resistant. This can reduce your reliance on pesticides and herbicides, including organic ones that may still have a negative impact on beneficial insects and soil organisms. Having an array of plants including drought-tolerant types also helps conserve water and reduce runoff, and it's more resistant to pests and diseases.

Plants that utilize nutrients more effectively do not require as much fertilizer, thus nutrients are distributed to other crops that need them. Plants with deep root systems limit soil fluctuations, help stabilize slopes, and maintain structure while robust varieties outperform weeds. Integrating fruit trees, berry shrubs or canes, as well as other perennial crops prevents soil erosion. Permanent crops provide constant harvests once established. In addition, flowering plants attract beneficial insects, both predators and pollinators, which contribute to plant vigor and improved crop yields.

SQUARE FOOT GARDENING

Square foot gardening is an intensive technique that entails growing different types of crops closely together. Plants adjacent to one another serve as a living mulch to block weeds and conserve moisture. It can be applied to in-ground or raised bed gardens to maximize space and productivity as well as boost yields. Every square foot is planted with a specific number of crops, each differing from the rest. Plant tall crops toward the back of the bed to prevent casting shade on smaller varieties. In summer, the canopies of tall plants will provide dappled shade for leafy greens such as lettuce and chard. See the following table for suggestions of the number of crops to plant in each square foot.

SQUARE FOOT GARDEN SPACING

The number of plants per square foot is based on their mature size.

PLANT	PLANTS PER SQUARE FT
Basil	2-4
Beet	9
Broccoli	1
Bush Bean	9
Bush Peas	9
Cabbage	1
Carrot	16
Chard	4
Chives	1 clump, 8-10 bulbs
Cucumber	1 per 2 sq ft
Eggplant	1
Garlic	9
Kale	1-2
Lettuce	4
Marigold	4
Melon	1 per 2 sq ft
Onion	9
Oregano	1
Parsley	2
Peas and Beans, vining	6 on a trellis
Pepper	1
Potato	1
Radish	16
Rosemary	1
Sage	1
Scallion	9
Spinach	9
Squash	1 per 2 sq ft
Strawberry	1
Tomato (determinate)	1
Tomato (indeterminate)	1 per 2 sq ft

ROW PLANTING

Planting in straight rows is a traditional way of growing crops. While it looks clean and organized, spaces between rows aren't used efficiently and are more likely to allow weed propagation. Intercropping between rows makes good use of vacant areas. For example, plant annual crops such as spinach or lettuce between open rows of perennial garlic (normally grown as an annual) for their mutual benefit. Garlic is a great companion plant known for naturally repelling insect pests because of its pungent aroma and it may resist soilborne fungi due to its sulfur content. The lettuce and spinach act as groundcovers to keep the soil free from weeds while conserving moisture. Ensure rows are properly spaced to avoid overcrowding and allow airflow and sunlight to reach the plants. Row planting does work well with crops that need ample room including corn, potatoes, peppers, beans, cabbage, summer squash, and tomatoes.

SUCCESSION PLANTING

Succession planting effectively uses space and timing. Staggering planting dates is a great way to extend harvests and increase crop yields and availability for the duration of a growing season. Two or more crops are planted in sequence every two weeks and can be sown until 6–8 weeks before the first frost. Plants mature about a week or two apart making harvests accessible throughout the growing months. This technique works well with fast-growing varieties that mature in about 60 days or less. See the list on page 64. Succession planting can also be applied when harvesting leafy greens in various phases of development. An example is by broadcasting bok choy or lettuce seeds and picking the outer baby leaves from every other plant within 30 days of seeding. When each plant has at least 8 leaves, harvest 2–3 leaves per plant, eventually pulling or thinning to every other plant while allowing the rest to mature. Another example is implementing the cut-and-come again method, which can be done with leaf lettuces, Romaine, or bok choy.

Harvest the leaves by cutting crosswise about 3 inches (7.6 cm) above the soil and leaving the crown intact. The remaining crown will regrow more leaves. Succession planting works with other fast-growing crops such as spinach planted between beets. When it's time to pull the spinach, you can sow more beet seeds.

INTERCROPPING

Intercropping or interplanting is planting two or more crops in the same location or in nearby rows. The spaces on the surface of the soil and below are utilized more efficiently when slow- and fast-growing crops are cultivated. An example of intercropping is growing shallow-rooted and fast-growing crops such as lettuce planted between deep-rooted and slow-growing tomatoes. The mature lettuce will be harvested before the tomato plants require room. Another example is to grow radishes between rows of parsnips. Radish is a fast-growing crop and can be harvested within 21–35 days, while parsnips take about 100 days to develop. As the radishes are harvested (and removed), they'll leave room for the parsnips to grow.

Interplanting lettuce with sweet alyssum encourages natural pest predation, leading to a reduced number of aphids and other pests.

COMPANION PLANTING

Companion planting is the technique of growing different plants in close proximity to each other for a particular benefit. Some of the possible benefits include to maximize space, to increase pollination, to provide homes to beneficial insects, and the technique is sometimes used as pest management. Companion planting can also add nutrients to soil by growing nitrogen-fixing crops such as legumes. Legumes such as peas and beans are in a symbiotic relationship with a soil-dwelling bacteria called rhizobia. The rhizobia bacteria extract atmospheric nitrogen and convert it into a usable form, such as nitrates, that plants can use, and which are stored in root nodules. In return, the plants provide nutrients for the bacteria in the form of exudates consisting of sugars and starches that are secreted from its roots. When leguminous plants are cut back before they set fruit, the stored nitrogen is released into the soil to benefit nearby plants.

Planting onions and marigolds as companion plants has been shown to help deter onion thrips.

FOOD FOREST

My relatives inspired us to grow our own food forest, which has been an ongoing project. As you stroll their homestead, you'll notice crops cultivated beneath some of their cherry, dwarf apple, and pear trees. This includes a combination of perennial varieties such as herbs; perennial tree collards and kale; currant, blueberry, and jostaberry (*Ribes x nidigrolaria*) shrubs; sunchokes; garlic and elephant garlic; leeks and shallots; and strawberries.

You'll also see vining plants, including champagne grapes and runner beans, as well as potatoes. A few annual crops are left to self-sow, such as spinach, lettuce, beet, and bok choy. These are crops that thrive in dappled or part-shade.

Food forests have become popular in recent years and more gardeners are implementing this method. It mimics a forest, but it's cultivated with perennial edible plants. It's a self-sustaining system of growing food as there is no fertilizing, watering, tilling, pesticides, or weeding. Companion planting with nitrogen-fixing crops replenishes the soil while flowering plants summon beneficial insects and act as natural pest deterrents. This technique embraces the principles of urban farming and permaculture while emulating a woodland ecosystem. A food forest is a biodiverse and resilient way of growing food. The Beacon Food Forest located in Seattle, Washington, is the largest public food forest in the U.S. This 7-acre food forest boasts fruit and nut trees, berries, perennial vegetables, annual vegetables, fungi, and more.

EXAMPLES OF FOOD FOREST CROPS: 7 LAYERS

There are several layers in a food forest. This example has seven layers of perennial plants that thrive in the part-shade planted below the tree canopies.

1. **Large tree canopy**: Fruit, nut
2. **Dwarf, semi-dwarf trees**: Fruit, nut
3. **Shrubs, brambles**: Red huckleberry, currant, gooseberry, jostaberry, blackberry, raspberry, blueberry
4. **Herbaceous**: Tree collards, perennial kale, sorrel, radicchio, rhubarb, asparagus,

   Allium: Garlic, multiplier onion, walking onion, leek

   Perennial herbs: Lovage, sweet cecily, parsley, mint, tarragon, feverfew, chives, lemon balm, lemon verbena, thyme, golden oregano
5. **Tubers**: Sunchoke, yacon, oca, earth chestnut, horseradish, potato in mild climates
6. **Groundcovers (Herbs)**: Chamomile noble, creeping thyme, Corsican mint, wild garlic, nodding onion, alpine strawberries, claytonia, clover, watercress, wood sorrel, sweet violet (*Viola odorata*), English primrose, pansy, viola, fungi (mushroom)
7. **Vining, climbers**: Runner bean, grapes

MANAGING PESTS IN THE SPRING GARDEN

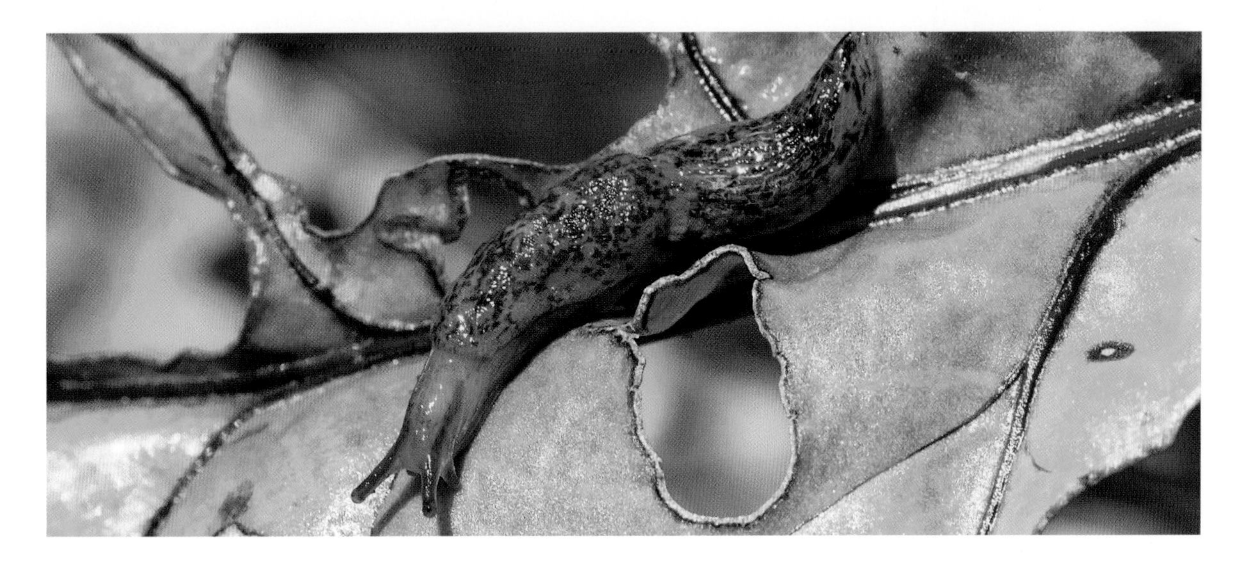

Wet and moist environments come with springtime and welcome garden pests. Gastropods such as snails and slugs are prominent in wet conditions. Besides consuming wilting plant remains and dead animal matter, they love to feast on succulent lettuce and cabbage leaves as well as ripe strawberries. Slugs and snails thrive in damp shady areas, and we often find them on surfaces hidden beneath leaves or mulch. They actively feed at nighttime so you may notice plant damage in the mornings. Pick up fallen leaves and remove any damaged, diseased, or decaying ones and compost them. Pick the older and lower leaves of lettuce and other leafy greens to open the spaces beneath, where slugs, snails, and wood lice tend to find shelter.

WOOD LICE

Wood lice, also known as pill bugs or roly polies, are crustaceans, cousins of crab, lobster, and shrimp. They have gills and need moisture to breathe; therefore, they thrive in moist environments. Wood lice can be found in damp soil, mulch, under rocks and pots, and in fallen vegetation. They consume decaying animal and plant matter as well as live plants and are known to remove heavy metals such as arsenic, lead, and cadmium from the soil. These toxins are crystalized and stored in their midguts. In most home gardens, they commonly feed on plant roots, strawberries, lettuce, carrots, grass, seeds, and seedlings. If there's plenty of decomposing organic matter, they're usually not bothersome, though if problems arise, they can be relocated by setting traps.

Left: To trap wood lice, place a piece of cut potato face-down on the soil. Check in the morning and use a trowel to scoop them up and place in compost pile or any other areas away from your garden.

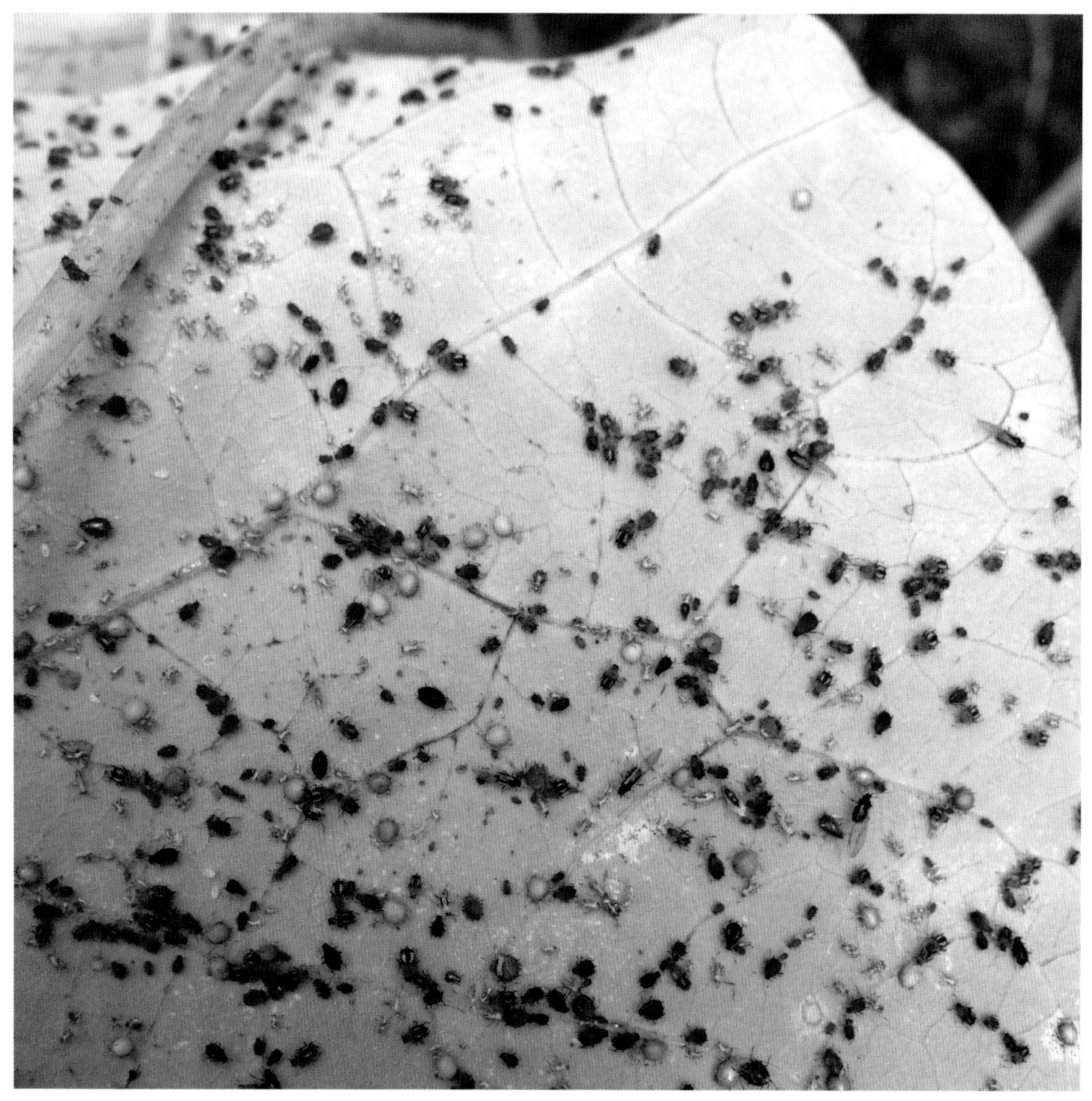

Try planting nasturtiums or borage a few feet away from potential host plants to deter aphids; This is also referred to as "bait or trap plants." Aphids will likely congregate on the bait plants instead of your crops.

APHIDS AND ANTS

Aphids are small, soft-bodied, sap-sucking insects that love to feed on plant juices of new succulent leaves, making seedlings vulnerable. Aphids are attracted to nitrogen. Overusing fertilizers can cause rapid growth in plants, which supplies aphids with more food to reproduce exponentially.

Spray aphids off plants with water; they have a hard time getting back up. You may find ants around if there are aphids as the two have a symbiotic relationship. Ants feed off aphid waste, called "honeydew," and will fend off attackers that prey on aphids. Remove the plants, prune off affected parts, or blast them off with water.

INVITE WILDLIFE

It's such a pleasure to hear songbirds; it brings us one step closer to nature. Your garden is an ecosystem filled with life, from tiny microbes in the soil to insects, lizards, frogs, birds, and small mammals. All living things play a vital role in the balance of our gardens and environment.

Invite wild birds to your garden by providing feeders, a bird bath, and/or a birdhouse. They're natural pest control and will devour pest larvae and other unwanted insects. You can also attract frogs or toads by leaving shallow, water-filled containers in shady areas or by installing a water feature. Frogs and toads eat slugs, snails, sowbugs, Japanese beetles, cutworms, cucumber beetles, and other garden pests.

On my morning garden walks, I inspect the brassica crops, which are a favorite of cabbage moths and cabbage looper larvae. I handpick and place the pests in a bowl that's left out for the birds to eat. Healthy and vigorous plants are most productive and less susceptible to disease and pest infestations. By providing the right environment and a balanced ecosystem, your crops will thrive and flourish and supply you with plentiful and tasty produce.

Right: Predatory insects such as lady beetles, lacewings, and soldier beetles help keep aphid populations at bay. You can attract these insects with flowering plants such as cilantro, dill, fennel, yarrow, marigold, sweet alyssum, and cosmos.

PRUNE OVERWINTERED HERBS

When pruning or pinching herbs, cut right above the lateral or axillary buds. If most of the stem internode is left it can rot and subject the plant to disease or pests.

Prune herbs in early spring just when they are starting to bud to rejuvenate healthy growth and maintain shape. Use a bypass pruner to cut back stems and foliage, especially diseased parts; remove any dead wood with an anvil pruner. Pruning or pinching growth tips will result in a bushier plant, giving you more foliage to harvest throughout the season. In our garden, several herbs are left to bloom for pollinators as well as other beneficial insects. Cut back spent flower stalks to promote new growth. Avoid pruning during rain as that can increase a plant's vulnerability to disease.

Cut back up to one-third of a plant to encourage new growth, but any more than that may stunt or be fatal to the plant.

MAKE YOUR OWN POTTING SOIL AND SEED-STARTING MIX

Potting soil and seed-starting mixes can be relatively expensive; however, with the right ingredients, you can easily make your own. Some store-bought potting mixes may contain chemical agents that you may not want if you grow organically. If you decide to make your own, wear a mask to avoid inhaling small particles.

DIY POTTING MIX

- Sphagnum Peat Moss: Decomposed sphagnum moss, which is harvested from peat bogs and runs acidic with a pH of 4.5.
- Coconut Coir: A byproduct of the coconut industry. Coir is the outer husk of coconuts.
- Perlite: Naturally occurring mineral or lightweight volcanic glass used to improve soil porosity, drainage, and prevent compaction.
- Vermiculite: Natural mineral with moisture and nutrient retention capacity that contributes to soil aeration.

DIY SEED-STARTER MIX

Mix thoroughly and add water to moisten. The consistency should be of a wrung-out sponge.

- 3 parts fine coconut coir
- 1 part worm castings

Or

- 1 part peat moss or fine coconut coir
- 1 part perlite
- 1 part vermiculite
- 1 part worm castings
- 1 tablespoon (15 g) garden lime per gallon (3.8 L) to lower pH of peat moss

DIY POTTING SOIL MIX

Combine all ingredients in a wheelbarrow or any large container and mix thoroughly.

- 2 parts coconut coir or sphagnum peat moss
- 1 part compost (add 1 cup [250 mL] worm castings to add extra fertility)
- 1 part vermiculite
- 1 part perlite
- 1 tablespoon (15 g) garden lime per gallon (3.8 L) if using peat moss

HOW TO PROPAGATE CHIVES BY DIVISION

Chive propagation can be done in early spring or fall. Over time, chives can lose robustness. Dividing them every three years will result in healthy and productive plants. You'll also have plants to share with family and friends!

1. Cut back chives about 1–2 inches (2.5–5 cm) above soil level.
2. Working your spade or shovel around the plants, dig and lift the clumps with the roots and bulblets intact. Try not to dig too close as you may slice and damage the bulblets and root system.
3. Carefully divide the clumps into sets of 8–10 bulblets.
4. Plant each set 8–12 inches (20–30 cm) apart or in a large pot (at least 12 inches, or 30 cm, in diameter). Cover the bulbs with soil, about the same depth they were originally in the ground or container.
5. Allow the plants to grow for several weeks. It usually takes 2–3 weeks to reach a height of 12 inches (30 cm).
6. Harvest with the cut-and-come-again method about 1–2 inches (2.5–5 cm) from soil level. Snip the tubular leaves 3–4 times in its first year and as much as every 4–6 weeks for established plantings.

TOMATO PROPAGATION FROM SUCKERS OR SIDE SHOOTS

Save a couple of suckers when you prune indeterminate tomatoes and propagate them to become clones of the mother plant. I prefer to have extra plants as back-up just in case some tomato plants perish due to early blight. Rooting tomato suckers is simple as tomato stems tend to form adventitious roots.

Notice the fine hairs on some plants such as tomato, sunflower, borage, squash, and cucumber? These are called "trichomes" and have specific roles that protect plants from adverse climatic conditions, stress, pests, and disease. Plant hairs do not develop into roots.

Root primordial (root nodes) occur on tomato suckers when immersed in water.

You may notice tiny nubs on stems of tomatoes and other nightshade plants. The plant hormone auxin initiates new root nodes, or root primordia, which is the earliest stage of root development. You may find these growing on non-root tissue where they are known as adventitious roots. I have seen these nubs on the lower portion on the central stems of pepper seedlings due to saturated soil from abundant rainfall and high humidity in late spring. The formation of root primordia is a plant's response to too much moisture in the air, overwatering, or stress conditions such as flooding, which can deprive roots of oxygen or nutrients. The bottom part of plant stems cut just below the axillary buds or nodes can be rooted when submerged in water.

HOW TO PROPAGATE TOMATOES FROM SUCKERS

1. Take a clean pair of scissors or snips and remove tomato sucker when it is at least 6 inches (15.2 cm) long. The sucker or side shoot grows in the leaf axil of a tomato plant, which is between the branch and the stem.
2. Place the sucker in water by submerging one-third of the bottom, plant it directly in a pot with moist potting soil, or in the garden.
3. Change the water every other day to prevent bacteria growth. Keep the soil moderately moist. In about 2–3 weeks, the suckers should have grown roots.
4. Plant in a sunny location spaced 24 inches (60 cm) apart or plant in a 15- to 20-gallon (57- to 76-liter) container.

5
SUMMER

The arrival of warm weather along with extended days and nights presents more time for us to spend in the garden. Have your checklist ready for completing daily tasks and harvesting—as well as enjoying—the fruits of your labor! It's great to be able to give some of the bounty to family, friends, and neighbors. We tend to grow an abundance of several crops so there's always extra to share. Summer mornings are filled with freshly picked crisp and buttery lettuce along with sun-ripened tomatoes bursting with flavor.

This is also berry picking season! Blueberries ripen between early and late summer depending on the cultivar. I really like 'Perpetua', which bears fruit in summer and fall. The berries are small but delectable and sweet! Harvest ripe strawberries before they become too soft and entice pill bugs, slugs, snails, or soil organisms as well as other animal nuisances. Aside from daily harvesting, inspect your crops when you are out and about for possible damage from garden pests and fungal or bacterial infection.

Raspberries and blueberries are picked daily. While some are munched by wild birds and squirrels, there are usually plenty to go around.

A technique I learned when I used to pick blueberries at a local farm is to cup your hand right beneath a clump of berries. Gently roll your thumb over the clump and ripe berries easily fall off.

Frequent herb harvesting by lightly topping off every few weeks will promote more vegetative growth instead of setting flowers. We allow a few herbs to bloom for pollinators. Keeping herbs pruned will also keep them tidy and shapely.

HARVEST NOW

Frequent harvests need to occur in summertime. Several crops continue to produce if they're picked regularly. If peas are left on the vine to fully develop and fill the pods, it signals the plant to halt flower production; harvest peas and beans often. The same goes for zucchini, which should be picked when they're 6–8 inches (15–20 cm) long. Fruit left for prolonged periods becomes large and won't be tender. Harvest cucumbers when they are still firm and green or dark green depending on the variety. Slicing types are ready for picking when they reach 7–9 inches (18–23 cm) long. Overdeveloped cucumbers will taste bitter and sometimes sour. They also turn yellow, become swollen, and may have wrinkled ends. If you'd like to save seeds, leave one or two fruits on the vine to mature later.

SECONDARY CROPS

Take advantage of secondary crops, which are other edible plant parts such as flowers, leaves, steams, or seed pods as well as the regrowth of existing plants such as lettuce or bok choy. On occasion, my parents would add squash flowers and bitter gourd leaves and tendrils to soups and stews. Squash blossoms have a mild flavor like squash itself and are delicious! When leaf lettuce is harvested with the cut-and-come-again method, you may harvest another round of greens before it bolts. It's important to get that last harvest before it sets flower buds as its leaves become bitter and unpalatable. Scarlet runner beans provide multiple crops such as flowers, young leaves and pods, tuberous roots, and mature beans that must be cooked thoroughly. Harvest edible greens from your root crops, too, such as beet, turnip, and carrot tops. Some foliage can be picked during root development and again when the roots are harvested. These are nutrient-dense and delicious! Carrot greens are strongly reminiscent of its taproot but with a higher nutrient profile. Turnip leaves taste like the root with mild peppery notes.

These Vegetables Produce Multiple Crops

- Bean: pods, beans, leaves, and flowers
- Borage: flowers and leaves
- Brassicas: flowers, leaves, tender seedpods, and stems (arugula, broccoli, cauliflower, kale, mustards)
- Cilantro: leaves, stems, flowers, roots, and seeds (coriander)
- Garlic: bulb, leaves, and scapes (flower stalk of hard-neck varieties)
- Leek and elephant garlic: bulb, scapes, and tender greens
- Nasturtium: flowers, leaves, and seedpods
- Onion, scallions, and shallots: bulb, scapes, and leaves
- Peas: pods, peas, flowers, pea shoots, and tendrils
- Radish: roots, flowers, tender seedpods, and leaves (cooked due to texture)
- Other root crops: roots and leaves (carrot, beet, and turnip; avoid parsnip leaves as they are poisonous)
- Summer and winter squash: fruit, male flowers, leaves (cooked due to texture), and mature seeds (roasted)
- Sweet potato (*Ipomea batatas*) but *not* conventional potatoes: tubers and edible leaves

Summer Harvests

- Bean
- Beet
- Berries
- Broccoli
- Cabbage
- Collards
- Cucumber
- Eggplant
- Garlic
- Kale
- Lettuce
- Melon
- Multiplier Onion
- Okra
- Onion, Bunching
- Onion, Walking
- Orach
- Pepper
- Potato (early season)
- Rhubarb
- Shallot
- Spinach, Malabar
- Summer Squash
- Sweet Corn
- Sweet Potato (warm climate)
- Swiss Chard
- Tomato
- Turnip

Summer Herbs

PERENNIALS

- Agastache (Hyssop)
- Bay Leaf
- Bergamot
- Chives
- Dill
- Echinacea
- Feverfew
- Lavender
- Lemon Balm
- Lovage
- Marjoram
- Mint
- Oregano
- Rosemary
- Sage
- Sweet Cicely
- Tansy
- Tarragon
- Thyme
- Wild Fennel
- Winter Savory
- Yarrow

ANNUAL AND BIENNIAL HERBS

- Basil*
- Borage
- Calendula*
- Chamomile
- Coriander (seeds)
- Lemongrass*
- Lemon Verbena*
- Marjoram*
- Parsley
- Summer Savory*

**Perennial in mild climates*

WHAT TO PLANT NOW

Direct Sow

Stagger plantings every 2–4 weeks for a continued harvest throughout the season. Try fast-growing crops that can be harvested within 60 days or less (see the following chart). Seed packets will generally state "days to maturity," which means the number of days from sowing seeds to harvest. Several early-maturing varieties fall between 45–60 days from seeding, but numerous greens can be picked within 30 days for baby leaves. Radish is a quick-growing root crop typically harvested in 21–35 days depending on the variety, although it prefers cool weather and should be planted in spring and fall.

SPEEDY SUMMER HARVESTS

The following summer crops are harvested within 60 days of seeding.

- Bush Bean: Sow every 2 weeks until 8 weeks before first fall frost.
- Sweet Corn ('Early Sunglow', 'Yukon Chief'): Sow every 1–2 weeks until 12 weeks before first frost.
- Cucumber (dwarf or pickling varieties): Sow every 3–4 weeks until 10 weeks before first fall frost.
- Summer Squash/Zucchini: Sow every 3–4 weeks until 8–10 weeks before first fall frost.

SUCCESSION PLANTING

Plant every 2 weeks for a continued harvest. Provide shade cloth for those crops that prefer cooler weather.

- Chard (baby greens)
- Kale (baby greens)
- Lettuce (heat-tolerant varieties: 'Paris Island Cos', 'Black Seeded Simpson', 'Oakleaf Looseleaf')
- Malabar Spinach
- Mizuna
- 'Red Giant' Mustard

Now is the time to start seeds for fall and winter crops.

Start Fall Crops Indoors or Outside

A sheltered location outdoors protected from afternoon sun makes an ideal place for starting seeds. We have a section protected by evergreen trees that receives morning and late afternoon sun where I start cool-season crops for fall and winter. I usually broadcast seeds into a raised bed, thin, and transplant into the garden as conditions allow. If you live in a relatively warm climate, starting indoors might be a better option to get seedlings off to a good start.

If you are sowing outside, use a lightweight row cover to shelter tender seedlings, keep the soil cool, and conserve moisture. Count back the number of weeks from your area's first frost date to allow adequate time for crops to mature. Some vegetables listed require 75 days or more to fully develop and should be started indoors. Note the time it'll take for crops to mature and start slow-growing vegetables indoors right away to ensure you get a harvest before the first frost. Plant transplants at least 6–8 weeks prior to the first fall frost date.

Fast-maturing and cool-season crops can be sown 4 weeks before your first fall frost or 2 weeks if you're growing under cover. Several cold-hardy crops can be overwintered with protection.

Sow Seeds from Mid- to Late Summer for Fall and Winter Picking

CROPS FOR FALL AND WINTER HARVESTS

- Arugula
- Beet
- Bok Choy
- Broccoli and Purple Sprouting*
- Brussels Sprouts*
- Bunching Onion
- Cabbage*
- Carrot
- Cauliflower*
- Chard
- Claytonia (Miner's Lettuce)
- Kale
- Kohlrabi
- Leaf Lettuce
- Mache (Corn Salad)
- Mustard
- Peas
- Radish
- Sorrel
- Spinach
- Tatsoi
- Turnip
- Walking Onions

**Start Indoors*

SUMMER PEST AND DISEASE MANAGEMENT

Powdery mildew is more prevalent during warm days and cool nights with high humidity. Late blight occurs when there's high moisture and moderate temperatures. This disease can destroy mature potato and tomato crops, making tubers and fruits inedible. It also affects other nightshade members such as eggplant and peppers, but not as severely.

Take preventative measures when plotting your garden and planting your crops. Ensure your garden receives adequate sunlight and has proper spacing between plants to allow airflow and prevent disease transmission. Disease-resistant varieties can lower the risk of running into problems. If a plant has any severely infected leaves and stems, remove them as soon as possible. Sometimes you may have to pull plants to prevent the spread of pathogens. As a precaution, discard any diseased vegetation and don't compost. Not all pathogens will be eliminated if your compost heap doesn't reach temperatures above 140°F. Fungal spores can overwinter and will be carried by wind under favorable conditions.

Common Diseases and Plant Ailments

Pathogens are transmitted by wind, insects, infected plants and seeds, contaminated tools, watering, and people.

Powdery Mildew: A fungal disease that proliferates on the tops and undersides of leaves caused by several fungi. Initially powdery mildew consists of white spots on the tops of leaves. Severe infection can lead to premature death of leaves and decline in fruit yield and quality. Powdery mildew infects cucurbits (melons, cucumbers, pumpkins, squash, and gourds), brassicas (kale, collards), and legumes such as peas, as well as numerous ornamentals .

Powdery Mildew

Early Blight

Early Blight: A common fungal infection affecting tomato and potato plants caused by *Alternaria tomatophila* and *Alternaria solani*. Initial signs are small dark spots, usually brown. Severe infection causes leaves to brown and fall off the plants.

Late Blight

Verticillium Wilt

Blossom End Rot (BER)

Late Blight: Caused by *Phytophthora infestans*, which commonly affects tomatoes and potatoes and can be devastating. First signs are large, dark brown blotches on leaves with greenish gray edges. Stems turn dark brown and round brown spots grow on the fruits, which turn mushy.

Verticillium Wilt: Destructive disease caused by the soil-borne fungi *Verticillium dahliae* and *Verticillium albo-atrum*. These pathogens commonly affect nightshade plants, squash, cucumber, several brassicas, watermelon, and pumpkin. Signs of disease include wilting of lower leaves with yellow spots which eventually turn brown and wither.

Blossom End Rot (BER): Physiological disorder due to calcium deficiency that may arise from soil moisture fluctuations or drought. It appears as a light brown spot at the end of the fruit, which becomes sunken as the fruit develops. The spot eventually turns black. BER affects tomatoes, peppers, and squash.

DIY BAKING SODA SPRAY FOR POWDERY MILDEW

Fungi thrive in mildly acidic to neutral environments with a pH of 5.0–7.0. Baking soda (sodium bicarbonate) has an alkaline state with a pH of 8 and works well as a contact fungicide. When sprayed on leaf surfaces infected with powdery mildew, it raises the pH, creating an unfavorable environment for mildew. This hinders colonization, kills spores, and thwarts spreading.

- 1½ teaspoons (7.4 ml) baking soda
- ¼ teaspoon (1.2 ml) dish soap
- 32 oz. (946 ml) water

Combine ingredients in a spray bottle and shake. Spray affected plants once weekly for 3 weeks. If problems persist, resume spraying. Remove heavily infected foliage.

PLANT DEFENSE MECHANISMS

Some plants have structural characteristics or barriers such as trichomes, thick leaves, spines, or thorns. Plants also produce phytochemical compounds that safeguard them from viruses, bacteria, and fungi. Through symbiosis, the beneficial mycorrhizal fungi that exist in the rhizosphere (area around the roots) assist plants to be more resistant to disease. When infestations are severe and something is out of balance, we may have to turn to pesticides, but it's best if we can avoid them. They are my last resort as we depend on beneficials to reduce insect pests and naturally stabilize the environment of our garden.

Neem oil and garlic sprays can be useful to control quite a few common insect pests including aphids, whiteflies (shown above), spider mites, scale, moth larvae, potato beetles, and thrips.

Natural Ways to Reduce Insect and Other Pests

As an organic gardener I avoid synthetic chemical pesticides. There are several disadvantages to their constant use. They are detrimental both to predatory and beneficial insects. Certain insects develop resistance to insecticides and the ones that survive may pass that genetic trait to following generations, causing an imbalance in the ecosystem. Extensive use of toxic chemicals is also harmful to wildlife and soil organisms, and it contaminates soil and groundwater.

Alternatives to inorganic pesticides include plant-based solutions and worm castings tea that can be purchased ready-to-use or made at home. Spraying plants with Neem oil and garlic barrier mixtures are effective and safer than chemical insecticides.

WORM CASTINGS TEA FOLIAR SPRAY

Healthy plants are less vulnerable to pests and disease. Using worm castings tea as a foliar spray introduces beneficial microbes, fungi, and nematodes as well as plant enzymes and hormones, all of which enhance plant growth and immunity. The microorganisms in worm castings tea dominate pathogens that may exist in the garden and deliver vital nutrients via leaf stomata. Research finds that worm castings contain an enzyme called "chitinase." This enzyme breaks down chitin, a compound found primarily in the exoskeleton of most insects. That's why worm castings tea is such a great repellant against aphids, spider mites, whiteflies, and other pests that feed on plant juices.

DIY WORM COMPOST TEA SPRAY

Mix 1 part worm castings tea from your worm bin run-off to 3 parts water and spray on the tops and undersides of leaves. If you don't have a worm bin, you may purchase vermicompost nutrient tea. For purchased nutrient tea, follow the directions on the package.

DIY NEEM OIL SPRAY

- 1 teaspoon (5 ml) cold-pressed Neem oil with azadirachtin
- 1 teaspoon (5 ml) dish soap
- 32 oz. (946 ml) water
- Spray bottle

Combine all ingredients in the spray bottle and shake. Spray affected plants 1–2 times weekly until insect numbers decrease.

NEEM OIL, A SAFER ALTERNATIVE

Neem oil is extracted from seeds of the *Azadirachta indica* tree, native to India. Cold-pressed Neem oil is comprised of a phytochemical called "azadirachtin." This substance interferes with an insect's endocrine (hormonal) system, which hinders feeding, growth, and reproduction, and works as a repellent.

DIY GARLIC SPRAY

- 4 cloves garlic or purchase liquid garlic extract
- 1 tablespoon (15 ml) vegetable oil
- 1 teaspoon (5 ml) dish soap
- 32 oz. (946 ml) water
- Spray bottle

1. Crush the garlic and place in a small bowl with the oil. Allow the oil to infuse overnight.
2. Strain the oil and pour into the spray bottle, add the soap and water, and shake.
3. Spray on the tops and undersides of affected leaves once weekly until problems cease. As a preventative, spray every 2–3 weeks.
4. For powdery mildew, spray once a week until it's eliminated. Remove heavily infected foliage.
5. Garlic barrier spray may deter rodents, rabbit, and deer too.

GARLIC, A NATURAL PESTICIDE AND FUNGICIDE

When garlic is crushed, its cell walls release enzymes that create a potent sulfur compound, allicin, that gives off a pungent odor. As the solution is sprayed, the extract is absorbed through the stomata or pores on the undersides of plant leaves. Due to its antifungal properties, garlic spray is also an effective treatment to prevent powdery mildew.

Insecticidal solutions should be sprayed before sunrise or in the evening when pollinators are not active. Don't spray in the middle of the afternoon as leaves can be scorched by sunlight. Avoid spraying plants adjacent to ones with a lot of pollinator activity. Spot test first on a couple of leaves and wait 24–48 hours to check for adverse reactions before resuming.

DIATOMACEOUS EARTH (DE)

Diatomaceous earth is comprised of diatoms, the fossilized remains of tiny marine organisms. Their skeletons are made of silica, which build up in the deposits of streams, lakes, rivers, and oceans where they're mined. DE is ground to a powder and can be inhaled accidentally, so it's a good idea to wear a mask when applying. The silica powder has sharp "edges" that make it effective.

Use DE to control garden pests such as cabbage worms and loopers, mites, aphids, flea beetles, ants, thrips, cutworms, squash bugs, snails, slugs, and cockroaches. Dust on plant leaves and stems and directly on insects. You can also spread the powder at the base of plants. Avoid getting DE on flowers as it can harm pollinators.

BIOLOGICAL PESTICIDES

Bacillus thuringiensis: *Bacillus thuringiensis* or Bt, is a soil-borne bacterium utilized as a natural insect pest control for various caterpillars. The bacteria produce crystal proteins that are consumed by insect larvae. The crystals dissolve within their guts and paralyze the larvae disturbing their digestive system and triggering them to stop eating. Bt isn't useful on mature insects and is generally used for larvae only. It's safe for organic gardening and doesn't harm humans or animals.

Beneficial Nematodes: Nematodes are soil-dwelling microscopic worms. Some species harm plants but some are beneficial and attack and feed on the larvae of several garden pests. Purchase the right type as specific ones target certain insect pests. The most common are *Steinernema* and *Heterorhabdtis*.

Apply *Steinernema* nematodes to control the larval stages of pests such as cutworms, armyworms, caterpillars, weevils, root maggots, thrips, cucumber beetles, corn earworm, and raspberry crown borer. *Heterorhabdtis* types can be used against Japanese beetles, Colorado potato beetles, flea beetles, and corn root worms. Nematodes may be sold at your local garden center or ordered online. Beneficial nematodes are safe for organic gardening.

Using Bait or Trap Plants

Spray aphids off plants with water. Try planting nasturtiums or borage a few feet away from potential host plants to deter aphids; this is also referred to as bait or trap planting. The aphids will most likely congregate on the bait plants instead of your crops. You can remove the plants, prune off affected parts, or blast off the insects with water.

Attracting Predatory Insects

Attract predatory insects such as lady beetles, lacewings, hoverflies, parasitic wasps, praying mantids, and soldier beetles by planting flowering plants to keep pest populations at bay. Some that we've had success with include cilantro, dill, fennel, yarrow, marigold, sweet alyssum, sweet cicely, candytuft, and cosmos. Members of the carrot family, *Apiaceae*, have been effective in our garden by attracting both pollinators and predators. See the sidebar on page 104 for a list.

Here, a lacewing larvae is ready to catch and devour an aphid.

PLANTS FOR BENEFICIAL INSECTS

These flowering species invite pest-eating beneficials and provide habitat.

Carrot Family (Apiaceae)

- Angelica (*Angelica sylvestris*)
- Anise (*Pimpinella anisum*)
- Caraway (*Carum carvi*)
- Cilantro (*Coriandrum sativum*)
- Dill (*Anethum graveolens*)
- Fennel (*Foeniculum vulgare*)
- Lovage (*Levisticum officinale*)
- Parsley (*Petroselinum crispum*)
- Sweet Cicely (*Myrrhis odorata*)

Cabbage Family (Brassicaceae)

- Candytuft (*Iberis*)
- Mustards (*Brassica juncea*)
- Radish (*Raphanus sativus*)
- Sweet Alyssum (*Lobularia maritima*)

Daisy Family (Asteraceae)

- Black-eyed Susan (*Rudbeckia hirta*)
- Calendula (*Calendula officinalis*)
- Chamomile (*Matricaria chamomilla*)
- Coneflower (*Echinacea*)
- Cosmos (*Cosmos bipinnatus*)
- Feverfew (*Tanacetum parthenium*)
- Shasta Daisy (*Leuchanthemum x suberbum*)
- Sunflower (*Helianthus*)
- Tansy (*Tanacetum vulgare*)
- Tickseed (*Coreopsis*)
- Yarrow (*Achillea millefolium*)

Imported cabbage worm.

Make Use of Row Covers

Cabbage white butterfly (*Pieris rapae*) larvae prefer cabbage and other brassicas. If you've grown cabbage, kale, collards, and other brassica crops, you might have witnessed white butterflies in your garden. They lay their eggs on the undersides of leaves, which later emerge as tiny green caterpillars. If you have hoops already installed, drape and secure a lightweight garden fleece over brassica crops. This physical barrier prevents insects from laying eggs, which breaks their cycle. This natural method works well, and dependence on insect repellents and sprays can be avoided.

Horticultural fleece is reusable and will last a few years if cared for and stored properly. Alternatively, row covers can be used to shade tender crops and keep the soil from overheating, which causes plants to bolt prematurely on very warm days. It's a natural process and the plant's way of reproducing. The leaves start to diminish as the energy focuses on seed production. Annual crops that are inclined to bolt are lettuce, arugula, spinach, and cilantro. Their leaves will taste bitter and become unpalatable. This can also happen to biennial crops including broccoli, cabbage and other brassicas, carrot, beet, leek, onion, and shallot.

SUMMER PLANT MAINTENANCE, WATERING, FERTILIZING, AND MULCHING

Watering the Garden

Vegetables need consistent moisture to be able to take up nutrients. Inadequate watering can lead to stressed plants and a lack of nutrient absorption, which increases the potential for disease and pests. Water deeply and less often; most plants require about 1 inch (2.5 cm) per week. If you live in a warm climate, your garden may need frequent irrigation. Test for moisture by placing your finger in the top inch (2.5 cm) of the soil; if it's dry, then water. Apply organic mulch to conserve moisture; mulch also keeps the soil and plant roots cool and suppresses weeds. Water early in the morning or in the evening to reduce moisture evaporation and avoid wetting foliage.

WHY LEAVES DROOP

As summer arrives, plants prepare to safeguard themselves from intense heat. While some show signs of distress now and then, other times it may just be a natural reaction to changes in the atmosphere. Plants may need water when their leaves start to wilt, but it's a good idea to check the soil for moisture anyway. Leaves may slump or look wilted even though they don't need to be watered. Waterlogged soil can prevent air circulation to the roots, which may cause them to rot and can be fatal. Often in hot weather, wilting leaves are a plant's natural response to high temperatures, extended periods of hot sun, and/or dry air.

Strong and frequent winds can cause leaves to dry out. Leaves droop to reduce surface area, which decreases water loss through transpiration. Occasionally plants drop leaves to lessen water loss when they're exposed to adverse conditions such as weather fluctuations. This can also occur during a transition in environment such as what happens when bringing in tender plants in fall to overwinter indoors where it lacks humidity.

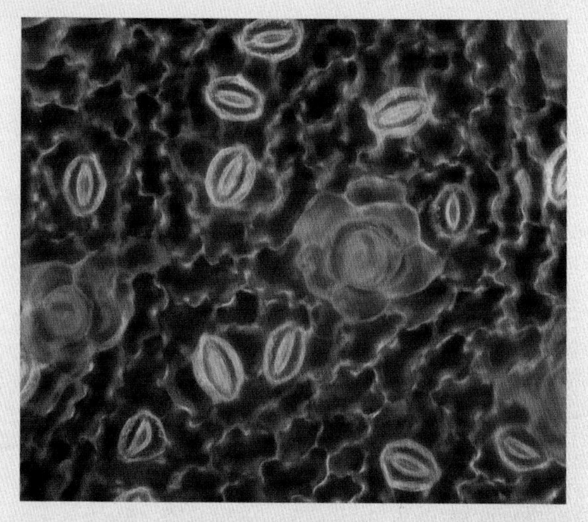

Leaf surfaces contain pore-like structures called "stomata." Their main function is to allow gas exchange. These pores also release water vapor into the air via transpiration.

Leaf curl is a physiological condition of tomato plants. Their leaves curl instead of droop when exposed to high temperatures or stressful conditions. Some varieties are more prone to developing it than others.

You may notice drooping leaves on newly transplanted seedlings as they slowly acclimate to their new home. If they're planted properly and cared for as you normally do, they usually recover within a few days.

Mulching

Mulch conserves moisture, acting as an insulator between plants and the soil; mulch can also prevent water that may carry pathogens from splashing up directly from the ground. Keep mulch away from tree trunks and the stems of shrubs and crops as doing so may encourage disease growth and provide a haven for garden pests. Avoid wetting plant foliage, which increases susceptibility to disease. Water potted plants until the water filters through the drainage holes. Soil in containers dries out faster, especially on warm summer days, which may necessitate watering in the morning *and* at night. Installing an irrigation system is a practical and cost-effective method that can lessen time spent watering.

Composting and Weeding

Continue building your compost pile or bins with your garden trimmings, lawn clippings, and kitchen scraps. Discard diseased plants. Warm weather speeds decomposition of organic materials. Keep your compost heap moderately moist to keep microbes and other organisms healthy and productive. Remove weed seedlings and their mature counterparts before they proliferate and add them to your heap. Avoid weed seeds in your compost pile as they may not get eliminated completely during the process and will likely sprout when conditions allow.

Pull weeds when the ground is moist early in the season or after rain when their pliable roots are easily removed.

Top garden beds with more compost before planting another round of late-season vegetables for fall harvests.

Fertilizing

Fertilize vegetables in containers every two weeks to support growth and production as nutrients are washed out when they're irrigated. Sidedress containers with your choice of organic fertilizer, lightly scratch into the soil, and mulch. Water thoroughly after fertilizing. Amend in-ground or raised bed gardens with a balanced fertilizer or organic compost every 3–4 weeks to support development and production. Crops can be sidedressed with a couple handfuls of compost or the recommended amount of organic fertilizer.

WHEN TO FERTILIZE PLANTS IN CONTAINERS

- **Leafy greens:** Every two weeks with diluted compost tea, sea kelp, or other liquid fertilizers. Or use a slow-release fertilizer or a couple handfuls of worm castings or compost every 3-4 weeks or as needed.
- **Tomato, pepper, eggplant, cucumber, squash:** Once every 2 weeks with diluted compost tea or liquid feed formulated for these plants.
- **Strawberry:** Biweekly with a balanced soluble fertilizer or liquid feed. If there's too much foliage growth and low fruit production, halt feeding.
- **Blueberry:** Once in early spring before leaves unfold and again in 2 months during its first season.
- **Blackberry:** Once in early spring with a slow-release fertilizer, then monthly with a balanced fertilizer.
- **Raspberry:** After initial feeding with a balanced fertilizer and aged compost or manure, there's no need to fertilize for about 3-4 months. Thereafter, monthly with a liquid feed such as worm castings tea or sea kelp.
- **Fruit trees:** Once in early spring and monthly with a slow-release fertilizer formulated for fruit trees.

**Don't fertilize in fall and winter as plants enter dormancy.*

FEEDING FRUIT TREES AND BERRIES

Fertilize fruit trees and berries in containers consistently during the growing season with a recommended balanced fertilizer. In-ground established fruit trees should have been fertilized in early spring and do not need additional amendments. Well-developed berry canes and shrubs grown directly in the ground require annual feeding in springtime.

SUMMER TIPS AND TASKS

HARVESTING, PROPAGATING, AND PRESERVING HERBS

Harvest from well-established plants; allow starts to establish for a couple of weeks or wait until they're at least 6 inches (15 cm) tall. It's important to harvest herbs soon after sunrise. The essential oils in leaves, which give herbs their aroma and flavor, peak early in the day. This is especially crucial when you're preserving herbs. Herbs contain the most essential oils right before blooming, which is a perfect time to harvest for drying. Prune flower buds as soon as they appear. Leaving them to bloom will hinder new leaf growth and cause herbs to taste bitter.

Harvest herbs every week or two by pruning the new growth tips to encourage the plants to produce more foliage and become bushier. Don't prune more than one-third of a plant. Simply pinch off the top 2–4 inches (5–10 cm) of new growth or down to the third or fourth set of leaf nodes.

Cutting back the growth tips directs plant hormones (auxins) to initiate the emergence of lateral buds, essentially waking them from dormancy and branching out into side stems. Two new stems will replace the one that's cut back.

When pruning or topping off, cut right above the leaf nodes, leaving no internodes. If an internode is left on the plant, it can rot or harbor disease.

The internode is the part between two nodes in a stem where nutrients, water, and plant hormones are transported within the plant.

HOW TO START HERB CUTTINGS

- Clean scissors or knife
- 4- to 6-inch (10- to 15-cm) pot
- Potting soil
- Cuttings

1. Using a clean pair of garden scissors, take 4- to 6-inch (10- to 15-cm) cuttings from new growth.
2. Make an angled cut at the bottom just below the leaf nodes.
3. Remove bottom leaves, flowers, and buds, leaving a few leaves on top. Reducing the number of leaves on cuttings prevents water loss (transpiration) from the leaves. Excessive water loss will cause the cutting to dry out as moisture cannot be replaced without roots.
4. Use a stick or a dibbler to make planting holes in moistened potting soil. Place cuttings into planting holes, about an inch deep. Press firmly around each cutting.
5. Place the pot in an area with indirect light. Keep the soil moderately moist.
6. Alternatively, cuttings may be started in water with their bottom inch (2.5 cm) submerged. Place in an area with indirect light and change the water daily to prevent bacterial growth. Plant cuttings when the roots are about ½ inch (1 cm) long.

HOW TO DRY HERBS BY HANGING

- Clean scissors
- Twine or string
- Herb sprigs

1. Harvest 4- to 6-inch (10- to 15-cm) stems and shake off any dirt or debris. Quickly rinse in cool running water if necessary. Air dry on paper towels in a warm room with good ventilation. (I normally don't wash herbs due to our humid climate, which can cause them to mold.)
2. Remove the bottom leaves leaving about 1½ inches (3.5 cm) of bare stem.
3. Tie 5–7 sprigs per bundle to allow good airflow between stems.
4. Hang the bundles in a dark, dry area with good ventilation. Keep sprigs out of direct light as this can alter color and beneficial properties.
5. Dry 7–14 days.
6. Prevent dust from collecting by covering the bundles with brown paper bags punched with holes on the top edge of the bags.
7. Completely dried herbs will crumble. Don't crush the leaves until you're ready to use them; this releases the essential oils.
8. Store in an airtight container in a cupboard or any dark, dry, and cool place. Properly stored dry herbs will last up to three years.

HARVESTING LETTUCE SEEDS

These dried lettuce flowers are ready for their seeds to be collected.

Summer is a great time to save seeds and among the easiest is lettuce. Harvest lettuce seeds by rubbing the flowerheads between your hands over a bowl or tray. (You may want to wear gloves.) The flowers can also be brushed back and forth or in a circular motion against the palm of your hand, like a paintbrush. Some of the chaff, the white fluffy material, will end up in the bowl. Remove the chaff using a strainer to separate the seeds or by gently blowing them away. Store in an envelope or a tightly sealed container in a dark, dry, and cool place.

HOW TO HAND POLLINATE SQUASH

Using a small paintbrush, collect pollen from the anther of a male flower and brush over the stigma of a female flower, which is attached to an embryonic fruit. Or simply pick a male flower and remove the petals. Gently touch the male anther a few times onto the female stigma. The flower is now pollinated, and fruit should develop shortly.

PROPAGATE STRAWBERRIES FROM CROWNS AND RUNNERS

Summer is a great time to propagate well-established strawberry plants by crown division or by runners. Lateral crowns grow at the base of the plants. A strawberry plant propagates by growing runners (stolons), which develop roots and new plants (clones). Once a plant develops, it can be cut off from the runner, which dies back naturally.

Stolons are stems that grow below and above the surface. In strawberries, stolons are commonly known as "runners" that grow aboveground where new plants develop from nodes. The new plants are clones of the mother plant. Cut off the clones from the stolons once they root. You can also root an emerging bud in a pot of soil.

HOW TO DIVIDE STRAWBERRY CROWNS

1. Dig up mature plants and look closely at the lateral crowns.
2. Carefully cut apart the clump and divide the developed crowns with at least ½-inch (1-cm) diameter.
3. Plant crowns at the same depth and water thoroughly.
4. Allow newly planted crowns or clones from runners to establish their first season by removing all blossoms. This increases the yield in following years.

6
FALL

As daylight lessens, deciduous trees divert chlorophyll from their foliage into their branches, trunks, and roots to conserve energy and prepare for winter. This seasonal transition reveals the ephemeral hues of autumn. Red, yellow, and purple shades within the leaves were there all along, temporarily hidden by green pigment within the chloroplasts. Cooler temperatures gradually slow plant growth, but it's a great time to plant fall and winter crops. Sow seeds and plant seedlings several weeks before your first frost date. Allocate sufficient time for your new plantings to mature or establish before cooler temperatures arrive. This gives crops time to produce the sugars they require to tolerate low temperatures, making them hardy throughout winter. If you live in a mild climate, you may direct sow several fall crops including some fast-maturing ones and some that will winter over.

Your compost pile will slow but will continue to decompose with temperatures at 40°F (4.4°C) and above. By the time the weather warms in spring, you'll have a nice, finished heap of nutrient-rich soil amendment. Collect and pile dead vegetation from the yard and garden (but avoid diseased plants). Fall leaves are excellent and can be used as leaf mulch for your beds. Crush the leaves first to allow water to penetrate through the mulch layers.

A great thing about autumn is fewer insect pest infestations! If you live in a wet climate, you may run into slugs or snails. Inspect crops daily and remove them as you find them.

You may notice crops taste sweeter in cold months. This is due to plants' converting starches to sugars, which gives them the ability to withstand freezing temperatures.

HARVESTING NOW

Fall Crops

- Bean
- Beet
- Bok choy
- Cabbage
- Carrot
- Cauliflower
- Chard
- Claytonia
- Collards
- Corn
- Corn Salad
- Cucumber
- Jerusalem Artichoke
- Kale
- Kohlrabi
- Lettuce
- Oca
- Parsnip
- Peas
- Potato
- Pumpkin
- Radish
- Sorrel
- Spinach
- Summer Squash (mild climates)
- Sweet Potatoes (mild climates)
- Tatsoi
- Tomato (mild climates)
- Turnip
- Winter Squash
- Watercress
- Yacon

WHAT TO PLANT NOW

Plant fall crops started in summer at least 6–10 weeks before your area's average first fall frost date. This will give them enough time to adjust and mature before you harvest or try to overwinter them. Your transplants can also be planted under a low tunnel, in a greenhouse or a cold frame.

Direct Sow

The following crops are early maturing and can be sown directly 6–8 weeks prior to the earliest chill. Cold-hardy varieties will overwinter. With decreasing daylight and lower temperatures, plants will not grow as fast or at a steady rate. Allow enough time from sowing to the earliest harvest possible.

TRANSPLANT OUTDOORS	WEEKS BEFORE FIRST FROST
Broccoli	8-10
Brussels Sprouts	8-10
Cabbage	8-10
Cauliflower	8-10
Collards	8
Kale	6-8

Don't forget to plant any perennial herbs you propagated from cuttings at least 4-6 weeks before your first fall frost.

WHAT AND WHEN TO PLANT: DIRECT SOW

CROP	NUMBER OF WEEKS BEFORE FIRST FROST
Arugula*	6-8
Beet*	6-8
Bok Choy*	6-8
Chard*	6-8
Claytonia*	4-6
Cilantro*	6-8
Leaf Lettuce*	6-8
Mache (Corn Salad)*	6-8
Mustard*	4-6
Peas	8-10
Radish	4-6
Spinach	6-8
Tatsoi*	4-6

**Will overwinter*

Planting Garlic, Elephant Garlic, Leeks, and Shallots

Garlic and elephant garlic are arguably the most popular fall-planted vegetable crops, but fall is also a good time to plant leeks and shallots. Plant several weeks before your first average frost date. This allows the cloves and bulbs time to establish roots before winter dormancy. Shallots planted in autumn will provide fresh greens early in spring, and the bulbs multiply and mature a couple of weeks sooner than those planted in the spring.

HOW TO PLANT GARLIC

Garlic is usually planted in fall at least 4–6 weeks before the first hard frost. This gives the cloves time to develop roots. Garlic requires vernalization, or a chilling period, between 4–8 weeks with temperatures 40°F (4.4°C) and below. This process stimulates bulb formation and division.

1. Select varieties suitable to your climate. Hardneck types are well-adapted to cooler regions and softneck types perform well in milder climates. Certain cultivars of hardneck thrive in mild or warm areas, but the bulbs may not grow to their full potential size.
2. Purchase or order certified disease-free bulbs. Do not separate the cloves until it's time to plant to prevent them from drying out.
3. Plant the largest cloves and use the small ones for eating. Bigger cloves produce large heads and cloves.
4. Soil should be fertile, loamy, and well drained. Amend with compost or organic fertilizer before planting. Avoid areas where water can pool.
5. Plant each clove 2 inches (5 cm) deep and 4–6 inches (10–15 cm) apart with the pointed end up. Space rows 12 inches (30 cm) apart. Plant 4–6 cloves per square foot. If growing in a container, ensure it's at least 8–12 inches (20–30 cm) tall with a 12-inch (30-cm) diameter. You can fit 4–6 cloves in a 5-gallon (19-liter) pot.
6. Water after planting if soil is dry.
7. For cold climates, apply a 3- to 4-inch (7.5- to 10-cm) mulch layer such as chopped leaves, straw, or dry grass clippings. Mild regions benefit from a thin layer of mulch; about 1–2 inches (2.5–5 cm) should be adequate.

COVER CROPPING

Cover crops increase organic matter, improve soil structure, and reduce weeds and pests. Planting cover crops can mitigate nutrient loss, create soil microclimates, house and feed microorganisms, and enhance biodiversity. Cover crops are usually turned into the soil in spring several weeks before planting edible crops. The decomposing vegetation or biomass is known as "green manure"; it feeds the soil and microbes thereby releasing nutrients in forms available for plants to use.

Leguminous plants are commonly utilized as cover crops for their nitrogen-fixing capabilities. Legumes have a symbiotic relationship with soil-dwelling bacterium, rhizobia, making it possible to convert nitrogen gas into a usable form, which plants can use. To take advantage of the stored nitrogen in the root nodules, the plants must be cut back when they start to bloom. This prevents the plant from using stored nitrates for energy to develop seeds. Cover crops should be turned into the soil at least 4 weeks before planting to allow adequate time for decomposition.

LEGUMINOUS COVER CROP CHOICES

If you haven't grown the cover crops listed here, make sure to inoculate the seeds before sowing with a specific type of rhizobial bacteria. There are different strains for certain plants. The seed inoculant can be mixed with water to help it adhere to the seeds. Plant immediately after inoculating to prevent bacteria from drying out. The seeds are broadcast on prepared beds.

ALFALFA (*Medicago sativa*)

Perennial, drought-tolerant, and winter-hardy. Will tolerate temperatures down to -30°F (-34°C). Blades will be killed by hard frost, but the crown areas regenerate.

CRIMSON CLOVER (*Trifolium incarnatum*)

Hardy to 0°F to -10°F (-18°C to -23°C). Grows rapidly. Best to grow in fall in mild climates or spring in cool areas. Crimson clover produces a significant amount of vegetation. Intercrop to suppress weeds and add color with its bold red blooms.

Crimson clover cover crop.

These young cover crop seedlings are helping to stabilize the soil in this raised bed.

HAIRY VETCH (*Vicia villosa*)

A winter-hardy cover crop down to -25°F to -35°F (-32°C to -37°C). The roots continue to develop over winter and produce substantial vegetation. Hairy vetch decays fast and releases nitrogen quickly.

WHITE CLOVER (*Trifolium repens*)

Low-growing and tolerates shade; makes a great living mulch in orchards or fruit gardens. A perennial hardy to -40°F (-40°C).

SWEET CLOVER (*Melilotus officinalis*)

A winter-hardy biennial, to -40°F (-40°C) but may survive to -50°F (-45.5°C). Vigorous and grows in compacted and clay soil. Survives drought.

SWEET BLUE LUPINE (*Lupinus angustifolius*)

An annual hardy to 0°F (-18°C). Its strong and aggressive taproot can reach deep into soil for water and nutrients.

WINTER RYE (*Secale cereale*)

The most winter-hardy cereal grain, to -30°F (-34°C). Fast-growing and can germinate at 33°F (0.5°C). Its fibrous and deep root system penetrates soil to prevent compaction. Improves water infiltration and soil tilth.

GARDEN CLEAN UP AND MULCHING

Another task to tackle this season is to gather autumn leaves for mulch. Shred them first to allow moisture and air to penetrate through the layers when they're applied as mulch. This can be done by running a lawn mower over a pile of leaves. Check with family and neighbors; they may have leaves you can put to good use. Leaf mold is an excellent source of organic matter and adds nutrients to soil as it decomposes. Use shredded leaves to mulch perennial plants after the first hard freeze, typically below 28°F (-2.2°C). By this time, plants should be dormant. Any herbaceous plant foliage should have already died back, and plants acclimated to cold temperatures. Apply a 3-inch (7.5-cm) layer of mulch, keeping it 3–4 inches (7.5–10 cm) away from a plant's base.

A thick layer of mulch over root crops enables you to harvest the roots through the colder months.

Mulching Root Crops

Overwintering root crops is possible where winters are relatively dry with well-draining soil. Regions with wet winters may risk root vegetables rotting in the soil. A great thing about leaving root vegetables in the ground in winter is they can be harvested as needed; you don't have to find storage such as a root cellar or basement. Another upside to overwintering
in-ground is they taste sweeter in the cold months as the starches convert into sugars, which is essentially a plant's way of increasing its tolerance to frigid temperatures.

Cold-climate gardeners can extend root crop harvests through winter and spring by insulating beds with a thick blanket of mulch, such as shredded leaves or straw. After a couple of days of frost and before the ground freezes, trim the green leafy tops of root vegetables. Place 10–12 inches (25.5–30 cm) of mulch over the entire bed area including the outer perimeter extending to about 1½ feet (50 cm). This is a viable way to maintain optimal temperatures between 35°F–40°F (1.7°C–4.4°C) for underground storage. These root crops should overwinter fine when mulched properly: carrots, parsnips, beets, and turnips. Consider installing a mini hoop house over a mulched bed if you live in a very cold climate to avoid deep freezes. Place a plastic tarp or row cover on top of the bed to keep the mulch materials from blowing away in case of strong winds. Secure the tarp with large rocks, wood boards, or bricks along the edges.

FALL TIPS AND TASKS

PRUNE EVERGREEN HERBS

If you didn't get around to pruning perennial herbs in spring, autumn is another time to do it. Cut them back up to one-third of the plant's height. This should be done at least 4–6 weeks prior to your first frost date; otherwise, any new tender foliage will be killed by frost.

- Lavender
- Rosemary
- Sage
- Thyme (semi-evergreen, some leaves fall in cold climates)
- Winter Savory

Cut these herbaceous perennial herbs to the ground after their stems die back.

- Catmint
- Fennel (may overwinter)
- French Tarragon
- Lemon Balm
- Mint (may overwinter)
- Oregano (evergreen in mild climates)
- Pineapple Sage
- Yarrow

FALL TIPS AND TASKS

OVERWINTERING TENDER PLANTS

Before we put the garden to a sleep, there are a few more tasks you may have to complete. If you plan to overwinter tender crops such as peppers or semi-hardy citrus trees such as 'Meyer' lemon indoors, prepare and bring them inside before the first frost. If they're currently growing in a container, remove the top 2 inches (5 cm) of soil to get rid of any insects and eggs and replenish with new potting mix. Cut off any dead or diseased leaves and stems. Water thoroughly until it drains through and place indoors near a sunny window away from heating vents or drafts. Plants might lose some leaves due to changes in the environment and humidity levels, but they usually bounce back.

FALL TIPS AND TASKS

PEPPER PLANT POWER

Peppers are perennials that thrive year-round in warm climates and are usually grown as annuals in mild and cold regions. Overwintering peppers gives you a head start to the following season and in some cases, they are even more productive! Select the healthiest plants for the best results. Dig up your plant if it's not growing in a pot and place in a container big enough to fit the rootball; remove the top 2 inches (5 cm) of soil. Backfill with new potting soil.

Prepare your pepper for winter dormancy by removing both immature and ripe fruits as well as all leaves. Cut the plant back by half or up to three-fourths. Prune down to a few "Y" stems with nodes. Buds will emerge into side stems in spring so cut *above* the nodes. Place in a dry, cool place near a window away from vents or drafts where temperatures remain between 50°F–55°F (10°C–12.8°C).

FALL TIPS AND TASKS

PLANT MORE PERENNIAL CROPS

Plant these perennials 4–6 weeks before your first hard freeze. Place 2–4 inches (5–10 cm) of organic mulch to insulate them from temperature swings.

- Asparagus (dormant crowns)
- Chives (divide and plant)
- Elephant Garlic
- Garlic
- Jerusalem Artichokes (a few tubers can be left in the ground to overwinter; they'll sprout in spring)
- Multiplier Onion (divide bulbs and plant)
- Rhubarb (dormant crowns)
- Shallots (divide bulbs and plant cloves)
- Walking Onion (divide bulbs and plant)

Jerusalem artichokes can be planted in the autumn.

7
WINTER

Winter is a time to reflect and relax with a cup of coffee in hand as you cozy up next to the fireplace. This is a perfect time to review your garden notes or journal and look through a list of crops that performed well or poorly, as well as your favorites. Browsing through seed and plant catalogs is an enjoyable winter pastime, although check your seed inventory and test for viability first (see page 129). List new varieties that you'd like to grow. Consider cultivating a mixture of different plants, which creates biodiversity in the garden and can lessen insect and disease infestations while creating microclimates for low-growing crops that shade the earth. Selecting new crops will provide you with unique options—plus, it's exciting to try new vegetables! This downtime is a great opportunity to plan your garden and crop rotation.

Following the winter solstice, the days become longer with shorter nights; this is such an exciting time for gardeners eagerly waiting to feel the earth! Set up your grow station if you plan on starting seeds indoors. A shop light with fluorescent tube lamps will suffice; just be sure to purchase a lamp with a color wavelength that mimics daylight. You may want to try winter sowing, which allows you to plant seeds directly outdoors in repurposed containers. A clean milk jug or plastic juice bottle can act as a miniature greenhouse. This technique can save time, energy, and work without taking up space indoors or setting up grow lights and trays, plus there's less mess and it gives you a head start on the season. The seeds germinate when outdoor conditions are favorable and no hardening off is necessary. See How to Winter Sow Seeds on page 126.

Lastly, inspect your tools for possible damage or wear and make repairs or replace them. In this chapter we'll go over the necessary tasks to ready you for a new season.

While you're waiting for the seasonal shift, why not grow some microgreens indoors on a windowsill or under grow lights? These tasty immature greens are remarkably high in nutrients and antioxidants, much more than their mature counterparts, and can be harvested within a week of seeding. See the instructions on page 128.

WHAT TO PLANT NOW

Though you won't likely be planting new vegetables in your outdoor garden if you live in a cold climate, it's a great time to get growing using a technique called "winter sowing."

These juice bottles are filled with winter-sown seeds ready to germinate when the weather warms.

Winter Sowing

Winter sowing is a simple and practical method for starting seeds outdoors. Varieties that do well started this way are cold-hardy crops such as kale and other brassicas, chard, spinach, lettuce, and lamb's lettuce. Self-seeding plants are also good candidates as well as plants that require a chilling period, known as cold stratification. I usually wait to start warm-season crops such as tomatoes and basil until closer to springtime.

Milk jugs make great containers for winter sowing all kinds of seeds, including cool-weather veggies, herbs, and perennials.

HOW TO WINTER SOW SEEDS

1. Save milk jugs and other plastic containers such as juice and water bottles. The tops are left off for venting and to allow water to enter from precipitation or overhead irrigation.

2. Cut each container about two-thirds of the way up, leaving one side intact to create a flip top.

3. Fill the vessel halfway with premoistened potting soil or seedling mix. I find that potting soil retains more moisture than a seed-starter mix. You can add some vermiculite to the seedling mix, which increases moisture retention, or place a thin layer on top after seeding.

4. Sow a few seeds in each container, only enough that it can accommodate the plants as they grow. For example, a milk jug should be able to accommodate up to 4 seedlings in the transplant stage. Sow 8 seeds, 2 in each planting hole, following the directions on the seed packet. Seed depth should be 2–3 times the diameter of the seed.

5. Flip the top over and close with duct tape. It's not necessary to seal the container all the way around. The spaces between the top and bottom where the cut was made will permit venting as the weather warms in addition to the open top. For cold climates, placing tape all the way around will help retain heat and create condensation, which keeps the soil moist.

6. Place prepared containers in a south-facing area or where they'll receive the most sunlight.

7. Seedlings are ready to be transplanted when they are about 4–6 inches (10–15 cm) tall or when they have at least 2–3 sets of true leaves. Plant in larger containers or directly in the garden; no hardening off is necessary.

Late-winter seedings of cold-tolerant crops under row covers, inside cold frames, and in unheated greenhouses will also jump-start the season.

WINTER TIPS AND TASKS

HOW TO GROW MICROGREENS

Winter is a terrific time to sow and grow microgreens indoors for a taste of homegrown greens all winter long.

1. Use a shallow tray that's at least 2 inches (5 cm) deep with holes for drainage. You can purchase trays designed for growing microgreens or you can reuse plastic food containers. A second tray, an old pan, or a cookie sheet can be placed underneath it for bottom watering or for catching drips.
2. Fill a tray with premoistened seedling or potting mix, about ½ inch (1 cm) from the rim and tamp down. We use coconut coir and, occasionally, grow mats.
3. Sow seeds thickly and evenly on the surface of your growing medium and tamp seeds down with your hand or with another tray. For larger seeds and ones with a hard seed coat, soak for 12 hours before sowing to speed germination.
4. Spray or mist with water, but do not saturate. Mist daily or twice per day to keep soil moist.
5. Place the tray in a dark area with good ventilation to prevent mold.
6. No light is needed until the seeds germinate. Seeds will sprout within 3–7 days of seeding. As soon as you see shoots emerge, place the tray on a south-facing windowsill or you may grow them under grow lights. Place the trays 8–12 inches (20–30 cm) away from a light left on for 6–8 hours per day.
7. Bottom water as needed whenever the tray feels light when it's picked up, about every 3–4 days.
8. Harvest microgreens in about 1–3 weeks depending on variety and the size you prefer. We harvest ours right before they get their first set of true leaves, usually 10–14 days after sowing.
9. Use scissors to harvest the amount you would like to eat. Cut the immature greens about ½ inch (1 cm) above soil level. You may harvest microgreens all at once, but they must be refrigerated to keep from wilting.
10. Before storing, place your harvest between two paper towels and press the delicate greens gently to absorb excess moisture. Dampness can lead to mold, which will make them unsafe to eat. Store microgreens in a plastic bag or container in the refrigerator for up to 7 days; however, it's best to enjoy them right away for optimum nutrition.
11. For a continuous harvest, use succession planting. Start your second tray about a week after the first crop, then start a third tray a week later, and so on. The spent growing medium can be added to your compost bin or pile.

WINTER TIPS AND TASKS

TEST SEEDS FOR VIABILITY

1. Place 10 seeds on one side of a damp paper towel.
2. Fold the paper towel in half and place it inside a partially sealed plastic bag or container.
3. Check for germination in 3–7 days.
4. Count the seeds that sprouted and multiply that number by 10.

For example, assume 8 seeds sprouted: 8x10 = 80 percent germination rate. If rate is below 60 percent, it's best to order new seeds; you can still plant them, but you'll have to sow densely to increase propagation.

WINTER TIPS AND TASKS

CHECK CROPS UNDER COVER

If there's been persistent snowfall, check your cold frame or low tunnel. Accumulating snow may cause the tunnel to collapse and it can freeze, making it difficult to open a cold frame. While a blanket of snow can act as an insulator, it can also block daylight from entering the structures. A broom can be used to sweep off the snow. While you're out and about, check on winter crops, especially on very cold and snowy days. You can capture heat by putting stones, bricks, pavers, and water-filled plastic jugs inside your cold frame or low tunnel. These trap thermal mass during the day from daylight and release heat at night. In addition to capturing heat, a thick blanket may be placed over a cold frame followed by a plastic tarp whose edges are secured with boards, stones, or bricks.

WINTER TIPS AND TASKS

HARVEST WINTER VEGETABLES

Harvesting sweet and tasty root crops in the middle of winter is such a delight! I love the convenience of heading out to the backyard and gathering fresh ingredients. To harvest root vegetables, lift the layer of mulch and dig into the soil. Pull out the ones you need and replace the soil and mulch layer. Don't be surprised if you find the mulch frozen at times, but it's usually not worrisome as the vegetables in the ground are insulated nicely. Use the vegetables within a day or two of harvest as they don't store well long-term.

WINTER TIPS AND TASKS

GARDEN HOOPS AND PVC

Winter is a great time to prepare and construct structures to keep birds from eating your delicious berries. Obtain bird netting with an opening of at least ¾ inch (1.9 cm), which will allow necessary pollinators to enter. You can utilize any garden hoops you already have. Place the hoops over a strawberry bed or dwarf blueberry shrubs. Drape bird netting over the hoops just like a row cover and secure with clothespins or clamps. A low tunnel can be made from PVC pipes (see page 55) and placed over a framed raised bed draped with bird netting. The same structure can be applied to taller berry canes and bushes. Measure the height of the plants and purchase the correct length of PVC pipes (10–12 feet, or 3–3.6 m). A bit longer is fine as that will allow a few inches (roughly 7.6 cm) all around for growth. Drive rebar into the ground and fit the pipe over it. Bend the pipe over the bushes and affix onto another rebar on the opposite side, making an arch. Repeat every 2 feet (60 cm) along the row until you have an arch on both ends. Place bird netting over the arch frame. Secure the edges of the netting to the ground with landscape staples.

Structures like this keep birds away from ripening berries.

I would like to thank you for including me in your gardening journey. Like many things in life, gardening successes are honed with time, practice, and little bit of trial and error. If things don't go exactly as planned, don't get discouraged: The key is persistence and learning from our mistakes. By implementing the techniques I've compiled in this book, you will be well on your way to growing and harvesting delicious and nutrient-dense homegrown produce year-round!

The following section includes some of our favorite annual and perennial crops, as well as unique varieties that you may find joy in growing and appreciate as much as we do. I hope that this book has inspired you to pursue the garden you envisioned for yourself and your loved ones. Wishing you much success on your aspirations for your very own four-season food garden!

PROFILES OF FAVORITE CROPS

Over the years, we've introduced commonly cultivated crops as well as diverse varieties, both native and nonnative, to our edible garden. These are some of our favorite crops including cold-tolerant and perennial cultivars that can be grown year-round in temperate to cold climates with some protection. A few may sound unfamiliar, but I hope to introduce you to several beautiful and edible plants that you may enjoy!

Arugula

Arugula will thrive through winter and snow under row covers, a cold frame, or in a greenhouse.

ARUGULA	
Eruca vesicaria, Cabbage family, Brassicaceae	
Planting Time	Spring, late summer, fall
Planting Depth	¼ inch (6 mm)
Spacing	6 inches (15 cm) apart; rows, 10 inches (26 cm) apart
Sun	Full to part-sun
Soil	Loamy, fertile, well-drained; pH 6.0-7.0
Water	Moderate
Hardiness	Hardy, tolerates frost
Germination Time and Soil Temperature	5-7 days, 40°F (4.4°C)
Maturity	45-60 days
Size at Maturity	12 x 12 inches (30 x 30 cm)
Harvest	Pick lower leaves and allow plants to mature
Pests	Whiteflies, aphids, flea beetles, thrips, leaf miners, crickets, grasshoppers, ants

If you've ever purchased a mesclun salad mix from the supermarket, you may have noticed arugula leaves mixed in. If you're looking for a fast-growing and tasty green, arugula is an excellent candidate. It's also known as roquette or garden rocket, which suits the plant's quick-growing habit. Arugula reaches maturity in about 45–60 days, although its lower leaves can be picked as early as 30 days from seeding. Arugula is a hardy cool-weather crop and can be sown as soon as the soil is workable in late winter or early spring and again in late summer and fall. It overwinters in temperate climates and is generally frost-hardy. Plant arugula between late-maturing crops such as tomatoes, onions, cucumber, or carrots. By the time arugula reaches maturity, it can be harvested and the companion plants allowed to fill in the bed. Alternatively, the taller crops can provide a canopy to shade arugula as the weather warms. For continuous harvest, sow seeds every 2–3 weeks in rows, square foot gardens, or containers. The peppery, tangy taste of arugula adds a small punch of spice to salads, sandwiches, pizza, and burgers.

Wild arugula (*Diplotaxis tenuifolia*) is a perennial species hardy to -20°F (-29°C). This variety is a good groundcover, making it a great addition to perennial food gardens.

Asparagus

Asparagus is one of the first to emerge in springtime when their tender spears poke through the soil.

ASPARAGUS	
Asparagus officinalis, Asparagus family, Asparagaceae	
Planting Time	Spring
Planting Depth	Bury 2 inches (5 cm) deep on a soil ridge
Spacing	Trench: 12–18 inches (30–45 cm) apart; rows, 2–3 feet (60–90 cm) apart
Sun	Full sun
Soil	Loamy, sandy loam, fertile, well-drained; pH 6.5–7.5
Water	Moderate, 1–2 inches (2.5–5 cm) per week
Hardiness	Perennial, -30°F (-34°C)
Germination Time and Soil Temperature	3 weeks, 75°F (24°C)
Maturity	2–3 years
Size at Maturity	12 x 12 inches (30 x 30 cm)
Harvest	Cut the spears right above soil surface
Pests	Common asparagus beetles, spotted asparagus beetles, cutworms

Asparagus is a delicious and prolific vegetable that will produce for many years once established. Some are known to have lived for 15–20 years or more! Asparagus is a hardy perennial crop acclimated to cold climes or down to -30°F (-34°C). Asparagus can be grown from seed, but it'll take about three years for plants to fully grow and produce. Growing asparagus from crowns accelerates growth and maturity, leading to earlier harvests. If you grow from seed, start indoors 14–16 weeks before your last spring frost and slowly acclimate seedlings before planting outdoors. Asparagus are dioecious, which means there are male and female plants. Male plants are generally more productive and develop larger spears. Female plants utilize energy to produce berries; therefore, they're usually not as abun-

Asparagus plants or crowns are comprised of rhizomes (underground stems and lateral roots). The spears emerge in spring and early summer.

dant. Select varieties adapted to your region so they perform well. Besides the cold-hardy types, there are some heat-tolerant ones acclimated for warm regions. While many describe the flavor of this versatile vegetable between broccoli and mushrooms, I find it more like green beans and artichokes. It's rather bitter and tangy when raw, but it's delightful prepared with olive oil and a squeeze of lemon juice. It is also excellent roasted. We are currently growing 'Purple Passion', 'Jersey Knight', and 'Mary Washington'. Here are a few varieties suitable for warm and cold climates.

Heat-tolerant

- 'Apollo' (male and female, hybrid)
- 'Atlas' (male and female, hybrid)
- 'UC 157' (male and female, hybrid)

Cold-tolerant

- 'Jersey Giant' (male, hybrid)
- 'Jersey King' (male, hybrid)
- 'Jersey Knight' (male, hybrid)
- 'Mary Washington' (female, heirloom)
- 'Martha Washington' (female, heirloom)
- 'Purple Passion' (male and female, hybrid)

Allow 1- to 2-year-old crowns to leaf out. Asparagus spears develop into fernlike foliage and give plants time to establish. The plants will be more productive by their third season.

HOW TO PLANT ASPARAGUS CROWNS

Plant asparagus crowns in a sunny location with loamy or sandy loam soil. Mix organic compost with native soil. Asparagus tolerates a wide range of soil from slightly acidic to neutral to slightly alkaline.

1. Obtain healthy 1- or 2-year-old crowns.
2. Soak the crowns in water for 20 minutes.
3. Dig a trench 12–18 inches (30–45 cm) wide and 10–12 inches (25.5–30 cm) deep.
4. If planting more than one trench, space rows 2–3 feet (60–90 cm) apart.
5. Form a ridge at the center of the trench 3 inches (7.5 cm) below ground level.
6. Place each crown on top of the ridge, 12–18 inches (30–45 cm) apart, spreading the rhizomes and roots.
7. Cover the crowns with 2 inches (5 cm) of soil and compost and water in.

Bean

Garden beans are loved by most gardeners. We enjoy growing snap and shelling beans as well as runners. Snap beans are also known as green beans, which are harvested for their tender pods that start to swell while the beans are still relatively small. Shelling beans are left to mature and dry on the vines; they're harvested before frost. Shelling beans are cultivated for long-term storage but may be prepared when freshly harvested. Bush type beans are excellent for small spaces or containers growing up to 24 inches (60 cm) tall. Pole beans are usually grown vertically and can provide microclimates to crops below. Utilize that space beneath by intercropping chard or kale. Beans are a member of the legume family and convert atmospheric nitrogen into a usable form (nitrates) via inoculation by rhizobia bacterium. Inoculants can be purchased at your local garden nurseries or online. This is applied right at planting; follow the directions on the package.

BEANS	
Phaseolus vulgaris, Legume family, Fabaceae	
Planting Time	Spring when soil has warmed
Planting Depth	1 inch (2.5 cm)
Spacing	2–4 inches (5–10 cm) bush and pole types
Sun	Full sun
Soil	Loamy, fertile, well-drained; pH 6.0–7.0
Water	Moderate
Hardiness	Not frost hardy
Support	Stakes, trellis for pole beans
Germination Time and Soil Temperature	8–10 days, 60°F (16°C)
Maturity	Bush: 50–55 days, Pole: 65–85 days
Size at Maturity	Bush: 12–24 inches (30–60 cm); Pole: 10–15 feet (3–4.5 m)
Harvest	Pick pods before they swell; leave shelling beans on vines to mature
Pests	Mites, beetles

Varieties

Bush: 'Tendergreen' (50–70 days)
'Tenderpod' (55 days)
'Jade' (55 days)
'Purple Queen' (50–55 days)

Pole: 'Kentucky Wonder' (67 days)
'Blue Lake Stringless' (65 days)
'Purple Podded' (68 days)
'Lazy Housewife' (75–80 days)
'Romano Pole' (70 days)

Runner: 'Scarlet Emperor Bean' (80–85 days)

Green beans are among the most prolific warm-weather crops for the summer garden.

Beet

Fall beets can be wintered over in a cold frame, greenhouse, or under a row cover in mild climates.

Beets are known for their earthy and bitter taste, but you can counteract that flavor if it's prepared a certain way. We find that simple seasoning such as sea salt balances the earthiness (what some people may describe as tasting like dirt). We enjoy beets oven-roasted with olive or coconut oil and sea salt. Roasting brings out its sweetness as it caramelizes the sugars. Boiling can give beets a texture like potatoes. They can be eaten raw, grated in salads, pickled, or canned. Beets are grown for their edible roots and leafy greens. Beet leaves look like chard because they're related, but they're smaller. Foliage is considered a secondary crop that can be harvested when you thin seedlings as well as young outer leaves early in the season. Allow remaining leaves to mature as energy is necessary for the roots to develop. Beets are a fast-growing, cool-season root vegetable that are typically planted in early spring, late summer, and early fall. Seeds can be sown inside a cold frame or beneath row covers in early spring and will germinate as the weather warms. For a continuous harvest sow seeds every 2–3 weeks till midsummer. For fall and winter harvests, direct sow at least 4–6 weeks before the first autumn frost.

BEETS	
Beta vulgaris, Goosefoot family, Chenopodiaceae	
Planting Time	Early spring, late summer, early fall
Planting Depth	½ inch (1 cm)
Spacing	3-4 inches (7.5-to cm); rows, 12 inches (30 cm) apart
Sun	Full sun
Soil	Loamy, fertile, well-drained; pH: 6.0-7.0
Water	Moderate
Hardiness	28°F-32°F (-2.2°C-0°C)
Germination Time and Soil Temperature	5-8 days, 50°F (10°C)
Maturity	55-65 days
Size at Maturity	12-18 inches (30-45 cm) x 18 inches (45 cm)
Harvest	Greens and roots
Pests	Leaf miners, leaf hoppers, flea beetles

Varieties

'Chioggia' (50-60 days)
'Avalanche' (50 days)
'Cylindra' (58 days, shaped like a thick carrot)
'Golden' (55 days)

Bok Choy

Extra-dwarf pak choi grows to about 2–3 inches (5–7.5 cm) tall (smaller than baby bok choy) and are ready to harvest in just 30 days. These tasty small cabbages are perfect prepared whole, steamed, and used in soups, salads, or stirfries.

BOK CHOY	
Brassica rapa subsp. *chinensis*, Cabbage family, Brassicaceae	
Planting Time	Spring and fall
Planting Depth	¼ inch (6 mm)
Spacing	8–12 inches (20–30 cm); dwarf: 4 inches (10 cm); rows: 12–18 inches (30–45 cm) apart
Sun	Full sun to part-shade
Soil	Loamy, fertile, well-drained
Water	Moderate
Hardiness	Tolerates light frost
Germination Time and Soil Temperature	4–8 days, 50°F–75°F (10°C–24°C)
Maturity	45–60 days
Size at Maturity	Standard: 12–18 inches (30–45 cm), dwarf: 6 inches (15 cm)
Harvest	Pick outer leaves or harvest with the cut-and-come-again method
Pests	Aphids, cabbage worms, cabbage loopers, cutworms, flea beetles, slugs

Bok choy was a regular ingredient in our household growing up. My parents chopped it and tossed it into soups, stirfries, and noodle dishes. The leaves have a mild cabbage flavor, and the stalks are crispy and juicy. We prepare bok choy pretty much the same way that my parents did, and our children enjoy it as well. Bok choy is a variety of Chinese cabbage that's also known as pak choi. It does not form heads; the leafy greens emerge from the white or lightly tinted bulbous bottoms. Dwarf and extra-dwarf bok choy are fun to grow and great for small spaces or containers.

Cabbage

CABBAGE	
Brassica oleracea, Cabbage family, Brassicaceae	
Planting Time	Start indoors 4-6 weeks before planting out or direct sow after last spring frost
Planting Depth	¼ inch (6 mm)
Spacing	18-24 inches (45-60 cm) apart
Sun	Full sun
Soil	Loamy, fertile, well-drained
Water	Moderate
Hardiness	Winters over
Germination Time and Soil Temperature	5-8 days, 70°F (21°C)
Maturity	65-180 days depending on variety
Size at Maturity	Varies
Harvest	Cut heads from stalks or pull the entire plant
Pests	Aphids, cabbage worms, cabbage loopers, cutworms, flea beetles, slugs

Cabbage is not just flavorful, it's exceptionally nutritious. It's a regular vegetable ingredient in our kitchen that's prepared a few times weekly. Cabbage is delicious raw, in salads, coleslaw, in stirfries, soups, sautéed, and cut into wedges and roasted. If you like sauerkraut, you can try fermenting your own at home. There are several varieties you can grow to your liking, whether you prefer the bold purple-red or mild types such as savoy, which have distinctively crinkled leaves. If you have a lot of space, various European heirloom types are stunning and remarkably large!

Cabbage plants are fairly cold tolerant and the flavor is sweetened by a few light frosts.

Early Maturing

'Earliana': 2 pounds (900 g), 60 days
'Early Golden Acre': 2-3 pounds (0.9-1.3 kg), 60 days
'Tendersweet': 3½ pounds (1.6 kg), 71 days

Late Season

'Savoy Perfection': 6-8 pounds (2.7-3.6 kg), 90 days
'Brunswick': 6-9 pounds (2.7-4 kg), 95 days
'Mammoth Red Rock': 8 pounds (3.6 kg), 100 days
'Late Flat Dutch': 10-15 pounds (4.5-6.8 kg), 105 days

Carrot

Late plantings are usually left in the ground under protection to winter over.

CARROTS	
Daucus carota subsp. *sativus*, Carrot family, Apiaceae	
Planting Time	Direct sow in early spring after soil has warmed
Planting Depth	Barely Covered ¼ inch (6 mm)
Spacing	2–3 inches (5–7.5 cm); rows, 12–18 inches (30–45 cm)
Sun	Full sun
Soil	Sandy loam, fertile, well-drained
Water	Moderate
Hardiness	Will overwinter
Germination Time and Soil Temperature	14–21 days, 55°F-75°F (13°C-24°C)
Maturity	60–80 days
Size at Maturity	Varies
Harvest	Loosen soil around roots with a garden fork and gently pull up
Pests	Carrot rust flies, wireworms

The first time we harvested homegrown carrots, our kids and I were amazed at how fragrant they were! Ever since, we've always looked forward to these juicy and kind-of-sweet garden-fresh taproots in summer. Before sowing, prepare the beds for planting. Ensure that the soil is loose and free of rocks and clods. If the soil is compacted, it may require tilling to a depth of 10–12 inches (25.5–30 cm); work in some organic compost too. Broadcast seeds thinly on a square foot or sow in a row ½ inch (1 cm) apart. Keep the soil moist to aid germination, which can take up to three weeks. Thin seedlings when they are about 1 inch (2.5 cm) tall, spaced 1 inch (2.5 cm) apart. As seedlings grow to about 4 inches (10 cm), thin once more to a final spacing of 3–4 inches (7.5–10 cm). Thinning prevents competition for water, nutrients, light, and space. Overcrowding prevents plants from developing to their potential. Carrot seeds can be sown successively every 3 weeks until 12 weeks before your first fall frost. Carrots are even tastier when they've been left in the cold because their roots convert stored starches into sugars. Mulch with a thick layer of straw a couple of days after a frost, but before the ground freezes, (8–12 inches [20–30 cm] of straw mulch for cold climates, 4–6 inches [10–15 cm] in mild areas). A floating row cover may be placed over for extra insulation.

Varieties

'Little Fingers', 57 days
'Parisian', 60 days
'Solar Yellow', 80 days
'Tendersweet', 75 days

Cardoon

Cardoon is unlikely to be in the produce section of most supermarkets here in the United States, but it is quite popular in the Mediterranean region. Although native to southern Europe and North Africa, cardoon has naturalized in California, South America, New Zealand, and Australia, and is considered an invasive species. Cardoon is also called artichoke thistle or wild artichoke and is closely related to globe artichoke. Both are members of the sunflower family. Cardoon is a stunning ornamental plant with grayish-green foliage covered with tiny spines, although spineless cultivars have been developed. Depending on variety, cardoon can reach a height of 5 feet (1.5 m) and a spread up to 6 feet (1.8 m). While globe artichoke is grown for its palatable flowerbuds, cardoon is cultivated for its flavorful and edible petioles, which taste like slightly bitter artichoke hearts. Bloom time is late summer between August to September. The prickly and vibrant purple flowerheads are showy and welcome pollinators including butterflies and bees. Preparation for cardoon's edible leaf stalks is time consuming, like that for artichoke flowers. The leaves are stripped off and the skin and ridges are removed. Cardoon stalks require blanching or overnight soaking to bring out their tenderness. They can be battered and fried or simmered. Because of their lengthy preparation, the stalks are a good alternative to celery in soups and stews.

CARDOON	
Cynara cardunculus, Sunflower family, Asteraceae	
Planting Time	Start indoors 6–8 weeks before planting outdoors. Can be winter sown or direct sow 3–4 weeks after the last spring frost.
Planting Depth	½ inch (1 cm)
Spacing	3 feet (90 cm); rows, 4 feet (1.2 m)
Sun	Full sun, part-shade
Soil	Loamy, fertile, well-drained, pH 6.5–7.5
Water	Low
Hardiness	Perennial, 0°F (-17.8°C)
Germination Time and Soil Temperature	7–12 days, 75°F (24°C)
Maturity	4–5 months after planting
Size at Maturity	3–5 tall (0.9–1.5 m), 4–5 feet (1.2–1.5 m) spread
Harvest	Edible leaf stalks
Pests	Mites, aphids, thrips, scab

Cardoon is primarily grown for its delicious leaf stalks, which have a flavor similar to the flowerbuds of globe artichokes.

Cauliflower

CAULIFLOWER	
Brassica oleracea var. *botrytis*, Cabbage family, Brassicaceae	
Planting Time	Start indoors 4–6 weeks before planting outdoors or direct sow after last spring frost
Planting Depth	¼ inch (6 mm)
Spacing	18–24 inches (45–60 cm) apart
Sun	Full sun
Soil	Loamy, fertile, well-drained; pH 6.0–7.0
Water	Moderate
Hardiness	Will overwinter
Germination Time and Soil Temperature	8–10 days, 65°F (18°C)
Maturity	55–80 days
Size at Maturity	12–30 inches (30–90 cm) tall, 12–24 inches (30–60 cm) spread
Harvest	Cut heads from their stalks
Pests	Aphids, cabbage worms, cabbage loopers, cutworms, flea beetles, slugs

Varieties

'Snow Crown' F1 hybrid: 60 days
'Cheddar' F1 hybrid (orange head): 75 days
'Purple Graffiti': 80 days

Cauliflower is a cool-weather biennial, although it is frost sensitive. To be honest, growing cauliflower has been challenging. It requires a consistent temperature and is finicky regarding weather fluctuations. The good news is the stems and leaves are also edible if the curd-like flower head does not form well. Cauliflower is best grown as a spring or fall crop with temperatures around 60°F–65°F (15.5°C–18°C); it suffers when air temperature is above 80°F (27°C). Keep the soil consistently moist or the flavor may turn bitter. Water at least 1 inch (2.5 cm) per week. If you prefer the flower head to remain white, fasten the lower leaves over the forming heads and secure loosely with twine or a rubber band allowing room for the developing heads. (Check your plants 30 days after transplant for emerging florets). This is called "blanching," and it blocks sunlight to prevent chlorophyll production so a curd retains its pale color.

Claytonia

CLAYTONIA	
Claytonia perfoliata, Family Montiaceae	
Planting Time	4–6 weeks before last spring frost, late summer to early fall
Planting Depth	⅛ inch (3 mm)
Spacing	4–12 inches (10–30 cm)
Sun	Shade, part-sun
Soil	Loamy, fertile, well-drained; pH 5.5–7.5
Water	Moderate
Hardiness	-10°F to -30°F (-23°C to -34°C) with protection
Germination Time and Soil Temperature	2–3 weeks, 50°F–55°F (10°C–12.8°C)
Maturity	40–45 days
Size at Maturity	3–8 inches (7.5–20 cm)
Harvest	Cut back to the top growth or down to two leaves and allow to regrow
Pests	Slugs

Miner's lettuce (*Claytonia perfoliate*) is also known as winter purslane and Indian lettuce. It's a common wild edible that's cultivated in home gardens too. Claytonia is native to Asia as well as coastal and western regions of North America from the southern part of Alaska to Central America and most notably, California. Its name was derived during the Gold Rush when Californian miners consumed its raw leaves for their abundant source of vitamin C to avoid scurvy. Claytonia is a nutrient-dense and cold-hardy leafy green. It may be grown as a perennial with winter temperatures -10°F (-23°C) and above. It can be planted as winter crop with some protection, such as a cold frame, in colder climates with temperatures down to -20°F to -30°F (-29°C to -34°C). Claytonia is a good addition to a permaculture garden or food forest and thrives in shaded and damp areas or in part-sun. The leaves and stems are crisp and tasty and are reminiscent of spinach; the flowers are edible too. Claytonia is a self-sower but it's not invasive. It thrives in most soil conditions, poor to acidic, neutral, or alkaline. Soil must be moist yet drain well; it will survive in dry soil.

Corn

Corn is a traditional summertime treat! It's even tastier freshly picked from a garden. The very first corn we grew was the beautiful 'Glass Gem' variety, which is adorned with multicolored kernels. It's more of an ornamental type but can be used as popping corn or ground into cornmeal. I didn't pay attention to its maturity date, so it was quite a long wait until harvest time, around 110 days. It was worth the wait since that was the first time we'd ever seen jewel-toned kernels! We used the ears to decorate our home through the fall holidays that year. We prefer sweet corn and like to grow early-maturing ones, which are more suited to our maritime climate. Corn is grown densely since it's pollinated by wind. The pollen from the tassels must land on the silks of the ears. Soak the seeds or sow directly 1 inch (2.5 cm) deep and 4 inches (10 cm) apart; thin to 8 inches (20 cm) when seedlings are 4 inches (10 cm) tall. Seeds should be planted in "blocks" instead of rows to ensure good pollen transfer.

CORN	
Zea mays, Grass family, Poaceae	
Planting Time	Spring as soon as the soil warms
Planting Depth	1 inch (2.5 cm)
Spacing	8 inches (20 cm)
Sun	Full sun
Soil	Loamy, fertile, well-drained; pH 6.0-7.0
Water	Moderate
Hardiness	Not frost hardy
Germination Time and Soil Temperature	5-8 days; 65°F-70°F (18°C-21°C)
Maturity	60-100 days
Size at Maturity	4-8 feet (1.2-2.4 m)
Harvest	Pick mature ears when the punctured kernels spurt pale liquid ("milk")
Pests	Corn earworms, cutworms, armyworms, flea beetles

Early Varieties

'Early Sunglow' hybrid: 63 days
'Spring Treat' hybrid: 68 days
'Spring Snow': 61–70 days

Late Season

'Bodacious': 75 days
'Golden Bantam': 82 days
'Ambrosia': 75 days
'Ruby Queen' (red): 75 days
'Glass Gem' (ornamental): 110 days

Egyptian Walking Onion

The bulbils can be separated and grown for individual plants. They have root nodes that anchor them to the ground.

EGYPTIAN WALKING ONION	
Allium x proliferum, Onion family, Amaryllidaceae	
Planting Time	Late summer or fall
Planting Depth	Bulbil: 1 inch (2.5 cm)
Spacing	6 inches (15 cm)
Sun	Full sun
Soil	Loamy, fertile, well-drained; pH 6.5
Water	Moderate
Hardiness	Perennial, -40°F (-40°C)
Germination Time and Soil Temperature	55°F (12.8°C)
Maturity	65–80 days
Size at Maturity	2 feet (60 cm)
Harvest	foliage, bulbils, bulbs
Pests	bulb mites, leaf miners, onion thrips, onion maggots, lesion nematodes

I am always on the lookout for vegetables that can be grown year-round. Egyptian walking onion, also known as tree onion, walking onion, and topset ting onion, is a cold-hardy perennial. It's one of the first to emerge in early spring, providing a harvest of green onions first and shallot-sized bulbs by summertime. It's quite interesting looking when the topset matures with a cluster of bulblets or bulbils supported by the stalks. The topset will continue to grow additional stems and start to look like Medusa's hairdo! It does not "walk" as its name implies, but when the stalk that supports the cluster of bulbils starts to die back, it topples over. Some bulblets that fall to the ground will root and grow. The reddish shallot-shaped bulbils are usually tiny, but I've seen some that grew to the size of a blueberry. Tree onion is a hybrid between the common onion and Welsh onion. Its flavor is similar to shallots but a bit more pungent. Harvest young leaf blades like chives and the mature ones can be used like scallions. The bulbils are great raw, pickled, or cooked, although I try to reserve them for propagation. The small onions can be prepared just like any regular onion bulbs. The whole plant can be lifted just as you would bulb onions, but it's a good idea to leave a mother plant or two to regenerate. Each plant will multiply over time to develop a clump of several plants that can be divided in spring. Separating the clumps and spacing them properly yields bigger bulbs. Like other onion plants they'll thrive best in full sun and in well-draining loamy or sandy loam soil. Bulbs should be planted in late summer to fall, which gives the plants time to mature by the following summer. If bulbs are planted in spring, they may not form topsets within that season. Given the right growing environment, you can have a patch of perennial onions for many years.

Elephant Garlic

Elephant garlic, *Allium ampeloprasum*, is also known as Oriental or great-headed garlic. While the bulb resembles a garlic, it's not a true garlic. It's considered a leek and has a mild garlicky flavor that's great in stirfries, soups, salads, and is wonderful roasted. The cloves and bulbs are usually larger than true garlic. It has the same growth habits as true garlic and develops a scape just like hardneck garlics. You may notice some bulbs produce yellow corms or bulblets that emerge from the basal plate, and look like miniature cloves. These can be left in the ground to self-propagate or remove them and plant elsewhere. The first season they'll develop into small, round bulbs like onions that can be harvested. If left for the following season they'll mature and divide into cloves. Basically, it takes two seasons for garlic corms to mature. Elephant garlic is cultivated the same way as true garlic.

Immature elephant garlic resembles a small onion. Spring-planted cloves form into these round bulbs.

ELEPHANT GARLIC	
Allium ampelopraum var. ampeloprasum, Onion family, Amaryllidaceae	
Planting Time	Late summer or fall
Planting Depth	2 inches (5 cm)
Spacing	6 inches (15 cm); rows, 12 inches (30 cm)
Sun	Full sun 6+ hours, tolerates part-shade
Soil	Loamy, fertile, well-drained; average pH 6.0-7.0
Water	½-1 inch (1-2.5 cm) average per week during growing season
Hardiness	Foliage is not frost tolerant
Germination Time and Soil Temperature	2-4 weeks, 55°F (12.8°C)
Maturity	7-8 months
Harvest	When one-third of the lower leaves turn yellow or light brown
Common Pests	bulb mites, leaf miners, onion thrips, onion maggots, lesion nematodes

Corms or bulbils develop on the roots of elephant garlic. Propagating from bulblets will generally take two seasons for the bulbs to mature and divide into segments.

Garlic

Garlic, *Allium sativum*, is a common ingredient in the kitchen due to its versatility and flavor. It's an excellent candidate for a perennial food garden. Garlic is commonly grown as an annual but it's a perennial. It's said that garlic has been cultivated for over 5,000 years, an ancient plant that originated in Asia where it can be found growing wild. We add fresh cloves almost daily to our meals. If you've never grown garlic before, it's absolutely worth the wait. We were inspired to grow garlic many years ago by my aunt and uncle and since then, it's become one of our favorite crops. Garlic is a beneficial crop that makes an excellent companion plant. It can repel garden pests because of its pungent aroma and sulfur content. It also has health benefits as garlic is known to possess antiviral, antibacterial, and antifungal properties.

GARLIC	
Allium sativum, Onion family, Amaryllidaceae	
Planting Time	Late summer or fall
Planting Depth	2 inches (5 cm)
Spacing	4–6 inches (10–15 cm); rows, 12 inches (30 cm)
Sun	Full sun 6+ hours, tolerates part-shade
Soil	Loamy, fertile, well-drained; average pH 6.0–7.0
Water	½–1 inch (1–2.5 cm) average weekly during growing season
Hardiness	Foliage is not frost tolerant
Germination Time and Soil Temperature	2–4 weeks, 55°F (13°C)
Maturity	7–9 months
Harvest	When one-third of the lower leaves turn yellow or light brown
Common Pests	bulb mites, leaf miners, onion thrips, onion maggots, lesion nematodes

Softneck

'Early Italian Purple': Attractive bulbs with purple vertical streaks. Matures earlier than most varieties; stores well; great for mild climates. Has mild flavor and pungent.

'Inchelium Red': Originally discovered in Inchelium, Washington, on the Colville Indian Reservation. It won the 1990 Rodale garlic taste test. Mild robust flavor and medium spiciness. Large bulbs and cloves have purple blotching. Stores 6–9 months. Adapts well to different climates.

Hardneck

'Music': Large bulbs and cloves with subtle, light purple hue. Cloves are easily peeled. Strong flavor with medium spice; performs well in cold climates.

'Russian Red': Excellent for cold climates as it is a very cold-hardy variety. Beautiful large bulbs with purple striped skin. Has strong and spicy flavor.

It contains a compound that may fight inflammation. As a companion plant, when garlic is planted adjacent to brassica crops (kale in this example), the rabbits leave them alone compared to ones that were not planted with it. As mentioned, garlic can be used as a barrier spray to repel other garden pests. There are two types of garlic: softneck and hardneck. Hardneck develops a flower stalk, or scape, followed by a flower bud and as the name implies, it has a woody stem. The bulbs are generally smaller, but they have bigger cloves. There have been times when we harvested hardneck bulbs that were much larger than the softneck varieties. Growing conditions and size of cloves planted play a role on end results. Softneck types don't produce a scape and have a flimsy stem that some gardeners like to braid. They're usually larger and produce more cloves. Softneck types store well and may last 8–9 months. Hardnecks generally last between 4–5 months depending on storage conditions. We grow both but we prefer the stronger and more complex flavor of hardneck types. Garlic requires vernalization, a chilling period, for the bulbs to form and develop. The cloves need at least 6–8 weeks of temperatures between 32°F–45°F (0°C–7°C). Selecting a variety adapted to your climate will increase success. Softneck types are well suited to and thrive in mild regions. Hardneck varieties benefit from exposure to cold winters. Order or purchase certified disease-free bulbs from reputable sources for the best results.

Keep garlic out of direct sunlight during the curing process as the sun's radiation can cause its flavor and beneficial properties to deteriorate.

Pick the scapes from hardneck garlic just as they start to curl. This diverts energy to producing robust bulbs. They are delicious sautéed with a texture similar to asparagus.

Scapes that are left on the plant eventually uncurl to point straight up and will produce bulbils, which are essentially clones of the parent plant. The size of a bulb will be significantly reduced.

Garlic is a perennial and can be left in the ground as a year-round crop. They'll regenerate in late winter or early spring when the soil warms. You can divide the cloves and replant them spaced properly. We keep a patch of perennial garlic for early spring greens and allow them to proliferate naturally.

HOW TO HARVEST GARLIC

I look forward to harvesting garlic and am excited to see the varying bulb sizes! Depending on cultivar and climate, you might be digging them up 7–9 months after planting. If your soil is loose, you can pull the entire plant up, but you risk damaging the neck, which should remain intact until they're dried or cured.

1. Using a shovel, garden fork, or hand trowel, lift the plant up, keeping your tool a few inches away from the bulb. Carefully remove most of the soil from the bulb.
2. Cure or dry garlic plants in a single layer away from direct light. You can use a wooden pallet as a drying rack, or hang in bundles of 3–6.
3. Make sure the area has good ventilation and airflow.
4. Curing may take 2–3 weeks or longer depending on temperature and humidity.
5. After drying, cut the stalks about an inch. Remove the outer papery skins and dirt and trim the roots to about ¼ inch (6 mm).
6. Store in a dry, cool area with proper air circulation at 50°F (10°C) or above. We store ours in woven baskets or mesh bags. You can store the bulbs loosely in a paper bag with holes, cardboard, or reused egg cartons. Braided garlic can be hung up and bulbs snipped off as needed.
7. Reserve the biggest bulbs for planting in fall.

Jerusalem Artichoke

Jerusalem artichoke, also called sunchoke, earth apple, sunroot, and wild sunflower, is a North American native. It's cultivated for its edible tubers or rhizomes. Sunchoke is a very cold-hardy perennial to -40°F (-40°C) and has adapted to cooler climates but it may be grown as an annual crop in warm regions. Jerusalem artichoke is related to sunflowers and blooms in late summer between August to September. The cheery yellow blossoms make lovely cut flowers. Harvest the rhizomes as needed or leave them in the ground through fall and winter. Exposure to cold improves the flavor of the tubers as the starches are converted to sugars. The tubers are knobby, similar to the appearance of ginger rhizomes, and appear in cream, pink, and reddish colors. Their interior may be cream, white, tan, and sometimes purple.

Sunchokes proliferate freely if allowed; give them their own space and plant in separate raised beds or large containers. Their flavor has been described a cross between artichoke, parsnip, and radish. Sunchoke is wonderful roasted in olive oil and fresh herbs as roasting brings out the sweetness. They're also delicious eaten raw for their crunchy texture. Peel and thinly slice the tubers to snack on or toss into a salad. They're great mashed like potatoes seasoned with Mediterranean herbs, olive oil, garlic, salt, and pepper. Sunchoke is a good source of inulin, a dietary fiber. Inulin is a prebiotic digested by our gut flora and may cause intestinal discomfort and bloating. For this reason, consider eating in moderation or cook them first.

JERUSALEM ARTICHOKE	
Helianthus tuberosus, Daisy family, Asteraceae	
Planting Time	2–3 weeks before last spring frost
Planting Depth	Tubers 4–6 (10–15 cm) inches deep
Spacing	12–18 inches (30–45 cm); rows, 18–36 inches (45–90 cm)
Sun	Full sun
Soil	Sandy loam, fertile, well-drained
Water	Low to moderate, drought tolerant
Hardiness	Perennial, -40°F (-40°C)
Support	May need staking
Germination Time and Soil Temperature	14–21 days, 50°F (10°C)
Maturity	120–150 days
Size at Maturity	7–10 feet (2–3 m)
Harvest	Late summer to fall
Pests	Slugs, swift moth larvae

The tubers have a mild yet sweet and nutty flavor with a similar taste to that of water chestnuts.

Its resemblance to the common sunflower is apparent in the blooms of the Jerusalem artichoke.

Kale

KALE	
Brassica oleracea, Cabbage family, Brassicaceae	
Planting Time	Start seeds indoors 4–6 weeks before planting outdoors; can be winter sown or direct sow after last spring frost
Planting Depth	¼ inch (6 mm)
Spacing	12–24 inches (30–60 cm); rows, 18–36 inches (45–90 cm)
Sun	Full sun to part-shade
Soil	Loamy, fertile, well-drained; pH 6.0–7.5
Water	Average 1–1.5 inches (2.5 to 3.5 cm) per week
Hardiness	10°F–20°F (10°C–20°C)
Support	Tree kale needs staking
Germination Time and Soil Temperature	5–14 days; 55°F (13°C)
Maturity	55–75 days depending on variety
Size at Maturity	Varies
Harvest	Harvest lower leaves to allow continued plant growth, leave terminal bud intact
Pests	Aphids, cabbage worms, cabbage loopers, root maggots, flea beetles

Another superfood that's packed with vitamins, minerals, and antioxidants is kale, a cabbage relative. Although it's a biennial, a certain number of developments have occurred through hybridization. Kale is typically grown as an annual and will set flowers the following spring. Occasionally they may flourish outside of their normal growth habits and stick around as a short-lived perennial. This was achieved by deliberately removing the side shoots and flowering stems through the year with the 'Tuscan' and 'White Russian' varieties, living for 3–5 years.

Numerous kale varieties are available and perennial ones are becoming more prevalent in many home gardens. Growing perennial kale will not require you to sow seeds every year if they're hardy in your climate. Allow young plants to establish by harvesting the lower leaves sustainably during their first season. Perennial kale is harvested the same way with the cut-and-come-again method for a constant harvest year-round. Plant them in full sun to part-shade with good soil and they'll give you plentiful harvests for years. Here are some perennial and biennial kale varieties that we currently grow.

Varieties

Sea Kale, *Crambe maritima*:
Sea kale, also known as scurvy grass, grows along the coast but it's not a seaweed; in fact, it's botanically related to cabbage. Romans preserved sea kale and brought it with them on their sea voyages to prevent scurvy as "scurvy grass" implies. Sea kale is native to Great Britain, growing wildly near the coast of the British Isles and continental Europe. Sea kale grows from tender spring shoots that have a faint hazelnut flavor. They can be harvested and prepared like asparagus. The leaves, stems, flower buds, and roots are edible, but the roots should be left so plants can reproduce. The leaves have a strong cabbage flavor, and the stems have a slightly bitter taste similar to traditional kale. They become tough over time. They can be eaten raw or cooked like other greens. Its ornate bluish green leaves and fragrant white blossoms resemble broccoli florets and add a dramatic display to any garden. Sea kale is a long-lived perennial reaching up to 36 inches (90 cm) in height and width; it can live to at least 10 years or longer. It is cold hardy to -30°F (-34°C) but may survive lower temperatures.

'Kosmic', *Brassica oleracea* (Acephala Group)
'Kosmic' kale is a bicolor variety with faintly curled blue-green leaves complemented by cream-colored margins. This is a stunning variety that can be grown as an edible ornamental plant in any landscape setting. 'Kosmic' grows to 24 inches (60 cm) in height and width and is hardy to 10°F (-12°C). This unique and beautiful variety is bred in Boskoop, The Netherlands, by Dick Degenhardt.

continues

'Homesteader's Kaleidoscopic Perennial Kale Grex', ***Brassica oleracea*** **var.** ***ramosa***
The magnificent 'Homesteader's Kaleidoscopic Kale Grex' was developed by interbreeding perennial bush kales, purple tree collards, and Daubenton kale. These were crossed with numerous kale varieties and other brassica members such as Brussels sprouts and cabbage. The result: a vast diversity of leaf colors and shapes. Colors range from green, variegated white and pink, dark purple, and yellow-green. The leaves appear ruffled, flat, wide, and long and thin. 'Kaleidoscopic Perennial Kale Grex' is hardy to 10°F (-12°C) and may grow between 24–36 inches (60–90 cm) in height and width depending on growing environment. This remarkable variety was developed by plant breeder Chris Homanics.

'Red Russian' Kale, ***Brassica napus*** **var.** ***pabularia***
This was one of the very first varieties of kale that we grew, to which we were introduced by our relatives. 'Red Russian' kale proliferated freely at their homestead and crossed with other kale plants resulting in hardier crops that grew as short-lived perennials. 'Red Russian' kale is an excellent variety; its leaves are tender and hold up to heat very well. While most kale turns bitter in hot summer weather, 'Red Russian' kale retains its mild and slightly sweet flavor. The leaves are flat and oak leaf-shaped with bold red and purple veins. We usually let a plant or two self-seed, which creates vigorous and resistant crops. This variety originated from northern Europe and Asia.

'Thousand Head Kale', ***Brassica oleracea L.*** **var** ***ramosa***
This French native heirloom is fun to grow for its size and beauty. Thousand head kale grows multiple side stems, the leaves are humongous, and plants can grow up to 5 feet (1.5 m), although some of ours topped nearly 8 feet (2.4 m) before they bolted. Our children call it the Jurassic kale tree! The leaves can grow up to 3 feet (90 cm), although so far, the longest we've seen in our garden was over 30 inches (76 cm) a few years ago. While the leaves get very large, they remain tender.

Lettuce

I always look forward to fresh crisp lettuce in early spring! We usually winter sow them to give us a head start to the season. They can be started in repurposed plastic containers or sown under cover. We also permit a couple of plants to mature in late summer and allow them to self-sow in a maintained area where we get volunteer crops. Lettuce is a cool-weather crop and is usually grown in spring and fall but will overwinter in temperate climates. They do well in full sun but thrive in part-shade, especially in summer. Plant lettuces beneath your tall crops so they're protected from afternoon sun. Consider growing heat-tolerant varieties, which are less likely to bolt, such as 'Red Oakleaf' and 'Parris Island Cos' Romaine. Providing a shade cloth can prolong your summer lettuce harvest.

Lettuces can be planted beneath tomato, bean, and cucumber vines, which will provide a microclimate. They can also be grown beneath sunflowers and corn stalks.

LETTUCE	
Lactuca sativa, Daisy family, Asteraceae	
Planting Time	Spring and fall
Planting Depth	Pressed into soil, less than ⅛ inch (3 mm)
Spacing	4 inches (10 cm) for leaf; 6–8 inches (15–20 cm) for heading; rows, 12–18 inches (30–45 cm)
Sun	Full to part-sun
Soil	Loamy, fertile, well-drained
Water	Moderate
Hardiness	Frost hardy but not for prolonged periods, or grow under cover
Germination Time and Soil Temperature	7–10 days; 55°F–65°F (13°C–18°C)
Maturity	Leaf varieties: 45–60 days; Heading: 80–100 days
Harvest	Pick outer leaves after 30 days for baby greens
Pests	Slugs, snails, aphids, leaf miners, root maggots, cabbage loopers, armyworms, corn earworms

'Marvel of Four Seasons' is one of our favorites and it's heat tolerant. It is a butterhead type with beautiful red-hued leaves that are succulent and tasty.

When sowing lettuce seeds, barely cover or press them into the soil. Lettuce seeds need exposure to sunlight as it helps break dormancy

Heat-Tolerant Varieties

'Batavian' (Crisphead)
'Black Seeded Simpson' (Leaf)
'Jericho Romaine' (Bred in the desert of Israel, very heat-tolerant)
'Little Gem' (Romaine)
'Lollo Rossa' (Leaf)
'Marvel of Four Seasons' (Butterhead)
'Oakleaf Looseleaf' (Leaf)
'Parris Island Cos' (Romaine)
'Rouge d'Hiver' (Romaine)
'Speckles' (Butterhead)
'Green Salad Bowl' (Leaf)

Oca

Oca, also known as New Zealand yam, is native to South America and a cousin of the common wood sorrel. It's an extremely prolific crop grown for its edible tubers, but all parts of the plant are edible.

OCA	
Oxalis tuberosa, Wood Sorrel family, Oxalidaceae	
Planting Time	Early spring when the soil is workable and has warmed
Planting Depth	3–4 inches (7.5–10 cm)
Spacing	12 inches (30 cm); rows, 18 inches (45 cm)
Sun	Full sun, part-shade in warm climates
Soil	Loamy, fertile, well-drained; pH 5.5–7
Water	Moderate
Hardiness	Perennial, 20°F (-6.6°C), foliage is frost tender
Germination Time and Soil Temperature	14–21 days, 70°F (21°C)
Maturity	6–7 months
Size at Maturity	12 inches (30 cm)
Harvest	Foliage will die back. Harvest tubers as needed, leaving some to winter over
Pests	Slugs, rodents

One plant can yield 30–50 tubers given the right growing conditions. The tubers' sizes range from 1–6 inches (2.5–15 cm) and are cylindrical or tubular shaped. Oca thrives in full sun in cool climates and in part-shade in warm regions. It's typically propagated by tubers like potatoes. Depending on variety, the tubers come in an array of colors including red, cream, white, yellow, and orange. Prepare tubers like potatoes including boiling, roasting, frying, grilling, or baking like candied yams—but they're great eaten raw. They taste like tangy potatoes or potatoes with sour cream! Oca is also described as tasting like sweet chestnut, celery, and apple. The leaves and flowers have a citrusy flavor and are good in salads. Oca is a perennial hardy to 20°F (-6.6°C) and it will overwinter underground. Provide a thick layer of straw mulch, row cover, or a cold frame to extend harvest by protecting the tubers. Oca contains oxalic acid, as do beets and spinach, and should be consumed in moderation.

Potato

Store potatoes in cardboard boxes with holes, baskets, or other containers that allow ventilation.

POTATO	
Solanum tuberosum, Nightshade family, Solanaceae	
Planting Time	Early spring, 3-4 weeks before last spring frost
Planting Depth	4-6 inches (10-15 cm)
Spacing	12 inches (30 cm); rows, 24 inches (60 cm)
Sun	Full sun, but tolerates part-shade
Soil	Loamy or sandy soil, fertile, well-drained, tolerates clay; pH 5.0-6.5
Water	1-2 inches (2.5-5 cm) per week
Hardiness	Annual, between 29°F-32° F (-1.7°C-0°C)
Germination Time and Soil Temperature	2-4 weeks, 40°F (4.4°C) and above
Maturity	60-135 days depending on variety
Pests	Potato leafhoppers, potato beetles, and wireworms

Potatoes are nutrient-dense and an excellent source of potassium. They contain good amounts of fiber, carbohydrates, and vitamins as well antioxidants. Our annual potato harvest is always exciting! I recall the first time we dug up our first potato crop—our children's eyes were wide open with surprise! It was like a treasure hunt for them. Since then, we've continued to plant tubers every season. Potatoes are placed in two categories, determinate and indeterminate. They are also classified by differing maturity times referred to as early, mid-, and late season. On average, early varieties mature in 60–80 days, mid-season mature in 80–100 days, and late season mature in 100–135 days. Most early and mid-season cultivars are determinate, which means the tubers grow in one layer near the seed potato, or mother plant. These kinds do not require hilling or mound-

Varieties

Early Season

'Yukon Gold': A yellow-fleshed tuber with golden skin. It has a buttery texture and rich flavor. Matures in 60–80 days, produces large tubers, and stores well. It's our favorite.

'Red Norland': Another early-maturing type that's ready in about 70 days. Tubers are large with red skin and white flesh.

Mid-season

'Red Pontiac': A main-season variety maturing in 80–100 days. Tubers have red skin with white flesh and are high yielding. Has good storage quality.

'French Fingerling': Large, delicious, rose-pink fingerling tubers with creamy yellow flesh. Matures in 80–100 days.

Late season

'Katahdin': A high-yielding late-season potato with buff skin and white flesh. It's drought-tolerant and has excellent storage life. Matures in 105–135 days.

'German Butterball': Medium to large potatoes with golden or yellow skin with brown patches. Tender, creamy flesh and a buttery flavor. Matures in about 90 days.

ing as the tubers are usually not exposed to sunlight. Indeterminate potatoes grow in multiple layers along the lateral stolons that grow along the main stem, which include late-season cultivars. These varieties should be mulched or hilled to keep the developing tubers covered. Exposure to sunlight will cause them to turn green and inedible. You can use straw, dry grass trimmings, or any other organic mulch to cover the tubers. They are ready when flowers start to fade or blossoms drop. The foliage will begin to die back and turn yellow as well. Harvest a few at time or as needed and allow immature tubers to develop more if you like. We usually wait to harvest until the tops of the vines die back to let the tubers store as much of the starch as they viably can. It's best to grow from certified disease-free tubers that are offered by numerous reliable vendors.

TRUE POTATO SEED, POISONOUS POTATO BERRIES

Not all potato plants develop the green berries that resemble cherry tomatoes or tomatillos. If you notice these, compost them and keep them out of reach of children and pets. These small green globes of fruit are high in solanine, making them inedible. Potato berries are mainly used by professionals to breed new varieties.

HOW TO CHIT POTATOES

Chitting, or sprouting, can help speed the growth and development of potatoes. It's a process that wakes the tuber from dormancy, making it ready for planting. Chit your potatoes 2–3 weeks prior to planting. Place tubers in a bright area or on a windowsill. A room with an ambience of 65°F–70°F (18°C–21°C) is ideal and should stimulate the eyes (nodes) to sprout.

HOW TO HARVEST POTATOES

1. Use a garden fork or spade and loosen the soil on the outer perimeter. Lift the plants.
2. Carefully remove soil on the tubers as you gather them. Don't scratch or damage the skin. Cure after harvesting to prolong storage.

HOW TO CURE POTATOES

The curing process toughens the skin, which extends the storage life of potatoes. Place tubers on a single layer on sheets of newspaper in a cool (50°F–60°F) (10°C–15.5°C), dark, and well-ventilated area. They will take about 2 weeks to cure; keep them out of light as they'll turn green. Gently remove any dirt and separate damaged ones, which can be eaten right away as they'll not store well long term. They should keep for several months at temperatures between 45°F–50°F (7.2°C–10°C). Store in a dark, cool area with good air circulation.

When potatoes are exposed to sunlight, they produce chlorophyll, which gives them a green color. Chlorophyll is harmless and is present in most edible plants we eat; however, its presence in tubers signifies that there is an increased production of a glycoalkaloid called "solanine." It's a phytochemical that's toxic in high amounts, which is why it's advised not to consume green potatoes

Radish

Some of our favorites include one popularly stocked in supermarkets called 'Cherry Belle', but we also like 'French Breakfast' and 'White Icicle.'

Radishes add a nice zest and color to salads and are great pickled or to snack on straight from the garden. They're easy to grow and mature quickly, some as early as 21 days! Besides the popular red globular taproots, radishes come in array of colors including pink, purple, green, yellow, and black. The flowers as well as the immature seedpods are tasty secondary crops! Radishes thrive best in cool weather and are usually grown in spring and fall, as summer heat will cause plants to bolt. Radish is an excellent crop to plant in succession due to its quick-maturing nature. Sow seeds every 10–14 days for a continuous harvest before the summer heat settles.

RADISH	
Raphnus sativus, Cabbage family, Brassicaeceae	
Planting Time	Direct sow 4–6 weeks before last spring frost
Planting Depth	½ inch (1 cm)
Spacing	2 inches (5 cm); rows, 12 inches (30 cm)
Sun	Full sun
Soil	Loamy, fertile, well-drained; pH 5.5–7.5
Water	Moderate
Hardiness	25°F (-4°C)
Germination Time and Soil Temperature	4–7 days, 50°F (10°C)
Maturity	21–35 days
Size at Maturity	6–18 inches (15–45 cm)
Harvest	Pull the whole plant and taproot
Pests	Cabbage root maggots

Rhubarb

Rhubarb plants are large so give them plenty of room. As you can see, mine have taken over a large part of one of my planting beds.

Our thriving rhubarb patch continues to flourish with vigor. What started out as young crowns now develop huge heart-shaped leaves, some with a diameter of 30 inches (76 cm) or more! A native of Central Asia, rhubarb is grown for its edible succulent and tart leafstalks, or petioles. The leaves are inedible because they contain significant amounts of poisonous oxalic acid, though leaves can be added to your compost heap. The zesty stalks make delectable savory jams and jellies, pies, crumble bars, and other baked goods. The variety we grow is 'Victoria', an heirloom with large, dark green leaves and tender, bright, red-tinged stalks. The flavor is a cross between a gooseberry and a tart apple. Rhubarb grows in most soil types: acidic, neutral, and alkaline. Soil should be moderately moist and well draining with plenty of organic matter. It thrives best in full sun but will tolerate part-shade. Rhubarb will multiply by sending new shoots from the crowns, which can be divided 5–6 years after planting. Split the roots in fall while they're dormant or in early spring as they start to bud and before they leaf out. Space each division 3–4 feet (0.9–1.2 m) apart in rows 4 feet (1.2 m) apart. Each plant can have a spread of 3 feet (90 cm) at maturity. Rhubarb is best if propagated from crowns as seeds aren't guaranteed to develop true to type.

RHUBARB	
Rheum rhabarbarum, Buckwheat family, Polygonaceae	
Planting Time	Early spring when soil is workable
Planting Depth	Bury crowns under 2 inches (5 cm) of soil
Spacing	4 feet x 4 feet (1.2 x 1.2 m)
Sun	Full sun to part-shade
Soil	Loamy, fertile, well-drained; pH 5.5-7.5
Water	Moderate
Hardiness	-40°F to -50°F (-40°C to -45.5°C)
Germination Time and Soil Temperature	Grown from crowns; 50°F (10°C)
Maturity	2 years from planting
Size at Maturity	2½-3 feet x 3-4 feet (70–90 cm x 0.9-1.2 m)
Harvest	Harvest sustainably in its second season when stalks are 12-18 inches (30–45 cm) long, ¾-inch (2-cm) diameter
Pests	Rusty snout beetles

Scallion

The scallion, also known as Welsh onion, green onion, or bunching onion, is a frequently used ingredient in most households. With a taste similar to its cousins, it's a versatile garden vegetable. Scallions are perennial bulbless onions with hollow tubular leaves. Due to its sulfur compounds, it can be planted throughout the garden to ward off aphids, flea beetles, and carrot rust flies as well as rabbits. Scallions are ready for harvest when they're 8–12 inches (20–30 cm) tall. The plants can be dug up or cut back to allow regrowth for a continuous harvest throughout the season. Cut plants back about 1–2 inches (2.5–5 cm) above soil level; they should regenerate with 2–3 weeks. Divide mature plants for propagation after the first season. Plant division is recommended every few years to encourage new, healthy growth. Separate the bulbs in springtime when the soil is thawed or in autumn. Welsh onion is hardy perennial to -10°F (-2°C), but other types may tolerate colder winter climes.

SCALLION	
Allium fistulosum, Onion family, Amaryllidaceae	
Planting Time	Early spring or can be winter sown
Planting Depth	¼ inch (6 mm)
Spacing	6–9 inches (15–23 cm); rows, 1–24 inches (2.5–60 cm)
Sun	Full, tolerates part-shade
Soil	Loamy, fertile, well-drained; pH 6.5–7.5
Water	Moderate
Hardiness	Perennial, -10°F (-2°C)
Germination Time and Soil Temperature	7–14 days; 60°F (15.5°C)
Maturity	60–90 days depending on variety
Size at Maturity	1–2 feet x 1 foot (30–60 cm x 30 cm)
Harvest	Cut plants back 1 inch (2.5 cm) from the soil surface or dig whole plants
Pests	Slugs, onion maggots, onion nematodes, thrips, leaf miners, cutworms

Scarlet Runner Bean

Scarlet runner bean, *Phaseolus coccineus*, is a tender, herbaceous, nitrogen-fixing plant in the legume family. They were originally cultivated in Central America and the mountains of Mexico and Guatemala for thousands of years. It's now grown in many parts of the world. The young immature pods are the sweetest I've ever tasted. The beans are brightly colored pink, mottled lilac, and black depending on the stage at which they're picked. They are almost too pretty to eat! This vining plant can grow up to 15 feet (4.5 m) in warm climates. Some develop tubers that can be left in the ground to winter over and grown as a short-lived perennial crop where winters are mild (lowest average temperatures in the teens). However, it's a good idea to apply a 4- to 6-inch (10- to 15-cm) layer of mulch for protection from hard frosts. The tubers can be dug up and stored in a frost-free location. They need humidity so they don't dry out. Place tubers in a pot with lightly dampened peat moss and set them in a dark, dry, and cool area. The foliage is not frost tolerant and seeds should be planted after the danger of frost has passed. Direct sow seeds 2 inches (5 cm) deep, spaced 4–8 inches (10–20 cm) apart, when temperature has warmed, (60°F–70°F, or 15.5°C–21°C). Keep the soil evenly moist; seeds will germinate in 7–14 days. The pods mature in 75–85 days from seeding. Consider isolating the plants from other legume varieties to prevent cross-pollination if you'd like to save seeds true to the mother plant. Most plant parts are edible, including the starchy tuberous roots, tasty flowers, young leaves, immature pods, and beans. As the pods fully develop, they become tough and are not so palatable as they become stringy. Mature beans need a good soaking and must be cooked

SCARLET RUNNER BEAN	
Phaseolus coccineus, Legume family, Fabaceae	
Planting Time	Spring, after soil has warmed
Planting Depth	2-3 inches (5-7.5 cm)
Spacing	4-8 inches (10-20 cm); rows, 24-30 inches (60-75 cm)
Sun	Full sun 6+ hours
Soil	Loam, fertile, moderately moist, well-drained; average pH 6.0-7.0
Water	Foliage is not frost tolerant, but tubers can overwinter with protection
Hardiness	Vining plant, trellis support
Germination Time and Soil Temperature	7-14 days, 60°F (15.5°C)
Maturity	75-85 days
Size at Maturity	Vines can grow 10-15 feet (3-4.5 m) long
Harvest	Pick immature pods (3-5 inches, or 7.5-13 cm), flowers, and young leaves; mature beans must be cooked thoroughly; edible tubers
Pests	Aphids, slugs, snails, cutworms, cucumber beetles

thoroughly. They contain lectin (phytohemagglutinin), which can cause gastrointestinal problems and other ailments. Scarlet runner bean is a versatile and attractive plant, making it aesthetically pleasing in the garden. Its beautiful flaming red flowers invite beneficial insects and attract hummingbirds.

The tubers of scarlet runner beans can be dug up and overwintered indoors before cold temperatures arrive.

Red-Veined Sorrel

Red-veined sorrel is as pretty as it is delicious.

RED VEINED SORREL	
Rumex sanguineus, Buckwheat family, Polygonaceae	
Planting Time	Early spring
Planting Depth	½ inch (1 cm)
Spacing	12 inches (30 cm); rows, 18–24 inches (45–60 cm)
Sun	Full sun, part sun
Soil	Loamy, fertile, well-drained; pH: 5.5–6.8
Water	Moderate
Hardiness	-30°F (-34°C)
Germination Time and Soil Temperature	7–21 days; 45°F–50°F (7.2°C–10°C)
Maturity	60 days
Size at Maturity	18 x 18 inches (45 x 45 cm), flower stalk: 30 inches (76 cm)
Harvest	Pick young tender leaves when they're 4 inches (10 cm) long
Pests	Slugs, snails, aphids

Red-veined sorrel, also known as bloody dock, is a decorative and cold-tolerant edible perennial. It's a cousin of French sorrel and native to Europe and Asia, but it can be found in certain regions in the United States and Canada. Its dark burgundy veins are an eye-catching contrast to its bright green ornate leaves. The leaves possess a sharp, citrusy flavor like other sorrels. The leaves are best harvested when they're young as they become tough upon maturity. Leaves can be consumed raw in salads or cooked like spinach. Sorrel is a great side dish for meat or fish, cooked with eggs, or added to soups. Red-veined sorrel is a hardy perennial to -30°F (-34°C) but it can be cultivated as an annual. Like its cousin, rhubarb, sorrel contains oxalic acid and should not be eaten in large quantities.

Swiss Chard

The multicolored 'Bright Lights' is a stunning mix with stems that come in crimson, gold, pink, white, orange, purple, and green.

Swiss chard, also known as perpetual spinach, silver beet, and spinach beet, is a biennial leafy vegetable and a cousin of beet and spinach. The gorgeous savoyed (crinkled) leaves come in an array of colors.

SWISS CHARD	
Beta vulgaris var. *cicla*, Goosefoot family, Chenopodiaceae	
Planting Time	Early spring, late summer, early fall
Planting Depth	½ inch (1 cm)
Spacing	12 inches (30 cm); rows, 18 inches (45 cm)
Sun	Full sun
Soil	Loamy, fertile, well-drained; pH 6.0–7.0
Water	Moderate
Hardiness	15°F -20°F (-9°C to -6.7°C)
Germination Time and Soil Temperature	5–10 days; 50°F (10°C)
Maturity	50–60 days
Size at Maturity	18–24 inches x 12 inches (45–60 cm x 30 cm)
Harvest	Leaves and stalks
Pests	Leaf miners, aphids

Swiss chard is a cool-weather vegetable although it's heat-tolerant and hardly bolts like spinach, making it an ideal green to grow through summer. Swiss chard will overwinter in temperate climates and bolt the following spring. The flavor of the foliage is enhanced by frost, but prolonged exposure to hard freezes will cause damage so it's grown as an annual in cold regions. The attractive, large, multicolored leaves of Swiss chard are decorative. Incorporate silver beet in container gardens with other greens such as kale and lettuce, and flowers such as nasturtium, coneflower, and carnation for a beautiful and edible display. The thick, succulent leaves and crunchy stalks of Swiss chard have a flavor very much like spinach and can be prepared the same way. Young and tender leaves can be picked within 30 days of seeding and are great with other salad greens. Like many other leafy vegetables, chard is delicious sautéed or stirfried.

Tatsoi

TATSOI	
Brassica rapa subsp. *narinosa*, Cabbage family, Brassicaceae	
Planting Time	Early spring
Planting Depth	¼ inch (6 mm)
Spacing	8–10 inches (20–25.5 cm)
Sun	Full sun, part-shade
Soil	Loamy, fertile, well-drained; pH 6.0–7.5
Water	Moderate
Hardiness	15°F (-9°C)
Germination Time and Soil Temperature	4–8 days; 50°F (10°C)
Maturity	40–50 days
Size at Maturity	8 inches x 12 inches (20 cm x 30 cm)
Harvest	Outer leaves can be picked within 3 weeks of sowing
Pests	Cabbage loopers, cabbage worms, flea beetles

This non-heading mustard is closely related to bok choy and puts on a beautiful display of crinkled, dark green, spoon-shaped leaves arranged in a rosette. Tatsoi is also known as rosette bok choy, spoon mustard, and spinach mustard. It tastes very similar to bok choy and grows quickly to give a harvest in just 3–4 weeks. Tatsoi is a cool-weather crop typically planted in spring and again in late summer to fall. It's a cold-hardy green and can overwinter under a hoop house, cold frame, or in a greenhouse. Exposure to cold enhances the flavor of the leaves. The leaves are delicious sautéed, added to soups, mix into green salads, or in stirfries.

Tomato

Ever since we started growing tomatoes, I have a hard time purchasing any at the supermarket. There's no comparison to homegrown produce, especially freshly picked vine-ripened tomatoes—they are exceptionally delicious! We've grown a combination of large and smaller kinds, but due to our mild climate we usually grow smaller varieties that ripen early. Tomatoes are categorized into indeterminate and determinate types. Indeterminate (vine tomatoes) will continue to grow and produce throughout the season until frost. They require support such as staking, trellising, or by containing them in a tomato cage. These varieties can reach up to 12 feet (3.6 m) in certain growing conditions. Some determinate and bush varieties top off around 4–5 feet (1.2–1.5 m). They usually don't need structural supports. This group includes dwarf and micro-dwarf types, which grow to around 6 inches (15 cm) tall. Determinate tomatoes produce one flush of fruit. Once fruits ripen plants start to lose vigor and will no longer produce fruit. These are great for limited growing spaces and do well in appropriately sized containers.

TOMATO	
Solanum lycopersecum, Nightshade family, Solanaceae	
Planting Time	Start seeds indoors 8 weeks before last spring frost
Planting Depth	Bury transplants with about two-thirds of the plant underground
Spacing	24 inches (60 cm); rows, 36 inches (90 cm)
Sun	Full sun 6+ hours
Soil	Loamy, fertile, well-drained, pH 6.0-6.8
Water	Averages 1-2 inches (2.5-5 cm) weekly; containers require more frequent irrigation
Hardiness	Not frost hardy
Support	Staking, trellis, cage
Germination Time and Soil Temperature	6-10 days, 70-80° F (21-27°C)
Maturity	50-100 days from transplant depending on variety
Size at Maturity	Determinate: up to 5 feet (1.5 m) tall; Indeterminate: up to 12 feet (3.6 m) tall
Harvest	Pick when fruit is uniform in color and still firm. Ripe tomatoes easily break off the vine with a slight twist. During hot weather, fruits can be harvested when they're still pink (red varieties) and allowed to ripen indoors where it is cooler.
Pests	Hornworms, aphids, stinkbugs, two-spotted spider mites, silverleaf whiteflies

Some favorites include 'Sungold', 'Roma', 'Early Girl', and 'Super Sweet 100'.

Indeterminate

'Sungold': A very popular sweet cherry tomato with vibrant golden orange skin. It's disease-resistant and matures about 60–65 days after transplant. 'Sungold' is a hybrid.

'Early Girl': Prolific and early producer of bright red 4–8 ounce (115–225 g) fruits; good flavor. Matures 50 days from transplant. 'Early Girl' is a hybrid resistant to verticillium and fusarium wilts.

'Striped German': Heirloom beefsteak type with medium to large fruits weighing 12–20 ounces (340–560 g). Beautiful and vibrant yellow and red marbled stripes. Great-tasting slicing tomato. Matures 78 days after transplanting.

Determinate

'Patio Tomato': A dwarf cultivar growing to about 2 feet (60 cm); produces flavorful 3- to 4-ounce (85- to 115-g) fruits. Patio tomato is a determinate bush-type excellent for containers no smaller than 5 gallons (19 L) (12-inch, or 30-cm, diameter).

'Roma': Roma is a plum type that produces 2- to 5-ounce (55- to 140-g) egg-shaped fruits with thick walls commonly used for canning (sauces and tomato paste). Roma is open-pollinated and is known to be resistant to verticillium and fusarium wilts. Matures 70–80 days after transplant. Great to grow in a 15-gallon (19-L) container (18-inch, or 45-cm, diameter).

Micro-dwarf tomatoes are fun to grow. 'Red Robin' tops at only at 6–9 inches (15–23 cm) tall and can be grown in a 6-inch (15-cm) pot. Its tiny red fruits are mild and tasty.

HOW TO PLANT TOMATOES

Many of us have heard the saying to bury your tomatoes deep! This is because tomatoes can form and develop adventitious roots along their stems (and even on the leaf stems). Burying tomato plants deep will anchor and keep them stable while the branching and vigorous root system supplies the plant with the nutrients and water it needs. A plant with a healthy root system is usually more productive and will have higher fruit yield and quality. Planting deeply can lessen a plant's vulnerability to drought.

1. Select a sunny location and loosen the soil 10–12 inches (25.5–30 cm) deep.
2. The planting hole should be deep enough so about two-thirds of the plant is buried and one-third remains on the soil surface. If your seedling is 10 inches (30 cm) tall, the bottom 6 inches (15 cm) would be buried and the remaining 4 inches (10 cm) of the stem is above the ground.
3. Amend the soil with your choice of organic soil amendment.
4. Remove the lower leaves and place plant into the planting hole. Backfill and firm the soil around the seedling.
5. Water thoroughly and keep the soil moderately moist. Lack of water or inconsistent watering may cause blossom end rot (BER). Be careful not to saturate the soil as it can lead to root rot.

HOW TO SAVE TOMATO SEEDS BY FERMENTATION

Saving seeds helps contribute to the plant's resiliency and adaptability to local growing regions or climes. It is also a way to be self-reliant as it gives you more control of the foods you grow and eat. You can save seeds from your best-performing, favorite plants and from unique or heirloom varieties. Plants that go through their lifecycle in your climate adapt to your growing environment; thus, they're more likely to do well, becoming hardy and more resistant to diseases and pests over time. We save tomato seeds using the fermentation method. This process eliminates any growth inhibitors and removes the gelatinous sheath around the seeds. Obtain seeds for saving from open-pollinated plants that didn't cross with another variety within the same species. Avoid seeds from hybrids as these will not breed true to seed (meaning, they will develop differently from the mother plant).

1. Select a ripe tomato and squeeze or scoop out the seeds into a jar or container.
2. You may cover the container with a paper towel secured by a rubber band or place a lid ajar to allow airflow.
3. Place the container or jar in a room with an average temperature of 68°F–72°F (20°C–22°C) and out of direct sunlight.
4. In about 3–5 days, you'll notice a layer of white mold on top. Scrape this off and fill the jar with water.
5. Stir the contents and allow to settle.
6. Carefully pour the water out and add more water and repeat until the pulp and nonviable seeds are eliminated.
7. Empty the water-filled jar and seeds into a strainer or fine sieve and rinse.
8. Allow the seeds to dry on the fine sieve, parchment paper, or coffee filter out of direct sunlight.
9. Store seeds in an airtight glass, metal, or plastic container. They can be divided into coin envelopes or plastic bags and then placed inside a tightly sealed container. Place in a dark, dry, cool place such as a basement or cupboard. If storing in a refrigerator, ensure that the seeds are completely dry to prevent mold.

Hybrid tomatoes such as the popular sweet cherry 'Sun Gold' is an F1 (Filial 1), hybrid, which means it has two different plant parents. As the first offspring of these plants, the seeds generally don't breed true to type or are sterile. This prevents the reproduction of a hybrid.

Tree Collards

TREE COLLARDS	
Brassica oleracea var. *acephala*, Cabbage family, Brassicaceae	
Planting Time	Spring, late summer, fall
Planting Depth	¼" (6 mm)
Spacing	18–24 inches (46 -61 cm); rows, 30 inches (76 cm)
Sun	Full sun 6+ hours, will thrive in part-shade (4–5 hours)
Soil	Loam, fertile, moderately moist, well-drained; pH 6.0–7.0
Water	Average 1–1.5 inches (2.5 to 3.8 cm) weekly
Hardiness	20°F (-6.6°C), provide winter protection, mulch layer, fabric cover in cold climates
Support	Stake at planting (Place a 3- to 4-foot, or 0.9- to 1.2-m, stake 2 inches, or 5 cm, from plants)
Germination Time and Soil Temperature	5–10 days, 45°F (7°C)
Maturity	12 months after planting
Size at Maturity	5–10 feet (1.5–3 m) tall
Harvest	Pick larger leaves, tastes sweeter when 40 percent of the leaf is purple
Pruning	Prune growth tips every 2–3 months to keep plants compact and dense, remove occasional flowers to promote leaf growth
Pests	Aphids, whiteflies, cabbage moths

In recent years, perennial tree collards, *Brassica oleracea* var. *acephala* have gained popularity in home and permaculture gardens due to their ability to produce abundantly year-round. They are low maintenance, heat tolerant, cold hardy, and more resistant to pests and diseases than most brassica plants. Other names include purple tree collards, tree cabbage, and tree kale. They are hardy down to 20°F (-6.6°C) and have been known to live more than 10 years in temperate climates; some have lived over 20 years. Tree collards are native to the Mediterranean, Africa, and the Americas and are closely related to other perennial collard variants.

Perennial purple tree collards.

The foliage is beautiful bluish green to purple and generally tastes sweeter than kale with a nutty flavor. The plant can grow up to 10 feet (3 m) tall or more with a spread of 6–8 feet (1.8–2.4 m) but can be kept as a tall shrub under 4 feet (1.2 m). It's usually more productive when its growth tips are constantly pruned back after harvesting. The nutrient-dense leaves are a good source of vitamins A, C, K, and B-6 as well as minerals such as calcium, iron, and magnesium. The foliage can be prepared like kale and collards and added to soups, salads, stirfries, pasta dishes, scrambled eggs, and even baked into chips with herbs and spices. Leaves can be blanched and frozen to use later or dehydrated and ground into powder to add to smoothies. We grow Purple Tree and Merritt Tree Collards from cuttings that I originally obtained from Project Tree Collard, a farm in Berkeley, California. Like most vegetables, tree collards thrive best in full sun, but can tolerate part-shade if they receive 4–6 hours of sunlight per day. The soil should be well draining and moderately moist with plenty or organic matter and a neutral pH of 6.0–7.0. Plant tree collards in spring after your last spring frost and when the soil has warmed.

HOW TO PROPAGATE TREE COLLARDS FROM CUTTINGS

Tree collards can be propagated from growth tips and branch cuttings any time of the year. In cold climates, do this 4–6 weeks before your first hard frost. They can be started indoors for planting out in spring. When taking branch cuttings, select new growth tips and non-woody parts of branches. You can get 3–4 cuttings from a branch; just select growth tips and branches with a diameter of at least ½ inch (1 cm). Cuttings should be at 6 inches (15 cm) long and most leaves should be removed except ones on top that haven't budded out completely. Removing leaves prevents transpiration (water loss) through its leaves. Each cutting should have at least 6 growth nodes. A growth node is the point from which leaves emerge or a scar when leaves are removed or have fallen off. The bottom of each cutting will be slightly curved; cut the top at an angle and leave the bottom flat so you know which side goes into the soil. You can also tell if the cutting is right side up by looking at a scar where a leaf was removed. The scar should have a heart shape or very similar if the cutting is held upright. Fill your containers or flats with quality potting soil, tamp it down, add more soil, and tamp again. Make sure containers are at least 3 inches (7.5 cm) deep. Poke holes in the soil and place the bottom half of each cutting into the holes; press soil firmly. Bottom water by submerging the flats or pots in a bucket or tray of water for a few minutes; remove when the soil is evenly moist but not saturated. Place cuttings near a window or in a room with indirect light. This will take 3–8 weeks depending on your climate; they root faster during warmer months. Don't let the soil dry out; check every 2–3 days and water as needed. After 3–4 weeks, you may notice leaf buds filling out as well as new leaves emerging on bare cuttings. Gently pull on a cutting; if it's not easily moved, most likely it's rooted. Start acclimating them for planting out in the garden. Follow the steps on how to harden off plants on page 59. Select a sunny or part-shade location. Mulch 1–2 inches (2.5–5 cm) around each plant. Mulching retains moisture by reducing evaporation while insulating the soil on cool days and keeping it cool on hot days.

Watercress

Watercress, or yellowcress, is a cold-hardy perennial from the cabbage family that's closely related to mustard.

Watercress is one of the oldest leafy greens known to be eaten by humans. It's a flowering aquatic plant that thrives along waterways such as streams. It has a spicy, peppery flavor like common garden nasturtium (*Tropaeolum majus*), although they're not in the same family. All plant parts are edible. Watercress spreads via rhizomes or stolons and will multiply freely. It's best to give watercress a space of its own or grow in containers for easier maintenance. When grown in pots, submerge the bottom in a tray or pan with 2 inches (5 cm) of water. As an aquatic species, watercress requires consistent moisture. The growth tips can be picked as early as 3–4 weeks from seeding. For mature plants, harvest by cutting back to 4–6 inches (10–15 cm) above the soil. Allow them to regenerate before the next harvest. Watercress can be grown as microgreens, which are harvested within 7–14 days.

WATERCRESS	
Nasturium officinale, Cabbage family, Brassicaceae	
Planting Time	Direct sow seeds 3 weeks before last spring frost
Planting Depth	¼ inch (60 mm)
Spacing	8 inches (20 cm)
Sun	Full sun
Soil	Sandy, loamy, heavy clay; pH 6.0–7.0
Water	High
Hardiness	Perennial, -40°F (-40°C)
Germination Time and Soil Temperature	5-7 days, 50°F (10°C)
Maturity	60–70 days
Size at Maturity	16 inches (40 cm)
Harvest	Leaves, flowers, stems
Pests	Snails, slugs, spider mites, whiteflies

HERB PROFILES

When we first started our garden, every now and then my mother would surprise me with an assortment of herbs that are still thriving and have been cloned a few times and shared with family and friends. Something about herbs' uniqueness and their distinctive aromas sparked my interest and inspired me to expand our herb garden. We have since cultivated several varieties, including numerous types of mint, throughout the backyard, which supply us with fresh as well as dried herbs year-round.

Growing herbs in a home garden serves several purposes other than culinary uses for their aromatic and savory properties. These versatile plants are not only aesthetically pleasing, but they also summon beneficial insects. Because of their fragrance, some work well to ward off insect and animal pests. Perennial herbs don't require yearly cultivation, which makes them easy to maintain once established.

Herbs are commonly grown for cooking as well as health and therapeutic benefits. Their foliage, flowers, stems, seeds, and roots can be used to create teas, syrups, herbal sachets, poultices, salves, infused oils, vinegars, and honey as well as tinctures. Herbs' essential oils are frequently extracted and added to personal care products and used in perfumery.

Herbs are great candidates for container and vertical gardening.

Bay Laurel

Bay laurel or sweet bay (*Laurus nobilis*) is an evergreen tree or large shrub native to the Mediterranean that is recognized as one of the oldest cultivated trees. It's hardy to 10°F (-12°C) and can be grown as a perennial in temperate climates or overwintered indoors in cold regions. The mature height can reach 25–55 feet (6.7–16.7 m) but can be kept compact by occasional pruning. Its beautiful glossy, smooth, dark green, oval-shaped leaves are often used to season foods. Leaves have a green herbal and floral note like thyme and oregano. Sweet bay is a common ingredient in our household. We use the leaves to season soups, stews, and a Filipino dish called "adobo." Young plants tend to grow slowly initially but they take off rather quickly once established. Bay laurel is an attractive container plant, but it should be repotted and the soil replenished every 2–3 years.

HOW TO PROPAGATE BAY LAUREL FROM CUTTINGS

The best time to take cuttings from bay laurel is midsummer when the stems are semi-woody but still pliable.

1. Take 6-inch (15-cm) cuttings from the end of a stem.
2. Remove the lower leaves to reduce water loss but leave the top two intact.
3. Make an angled cut at the bottom of the stem below the nodes.
4. Place the bottom 2 inches (5 cm) of the cutting in a pot with good-quality potting mix. Apply rooting hormone to the cut end first if you prefer.
5. Water and keep the soil moderately moist. Keep out of direct sunlight.
6. It can take up to two months or so, sometimes sooner, to root.

Roman Chamomile

Roman chamomile is the perennial variety that's considered the "true chamomile" and has similar uses to the annual type, German chamomile. Both are members of the sunflower family. *Chamaemelum nobile* is cold hardy to -30°F (-34°C) and has a creeping growth habit, topping around 3–6 inches (7.5–15 cm), and making a pretty groundcover or border with its small daisylike flowers. The flowers have white petals and yellow centers just like annual chamomile. The blossoms can be used fresh or dried to make a soothing herbal tea.

Chives

Chives (*Allium schoenoprasum*) is a perennial and a member of the onion family, Amaryllidaceae. It's closely related to leek, shallot, scallion, onion, and garlic. It's cold hardy to -40°F (-40°C) and thrives best in full sun although it tolerates part-shade. Chives is an excellent companion plant as its blossoms attract beneficial insects and pollinators such as bees, wasps, and butterflies. Due to the sulfur compounds within the plant, chives have a natural onion scent and may repel aphids, carrot flies, and Japanese beetles. The tubular-shaped foliage and flowers add great flavor to several dishes and can replace scallions or green onions. Its flowers are great in salads, blended with butter, or infused in vinegar for salad dressings or other recipes! Besides culinary uses, chives possess some health benefits. Because of chives' antifungal, antibacterial, and antiviral properties, it's said that it may boost the immune system, and improve skin, heart, and bone health.

Cilantro

Cilantro (*Coriandrum sativum*), also known as Chinese parsley, is an annual herb in the carrot family, Apiaceae. The whole plant is edible, including leaves, stems, flowers, roots, and seeds (which are referred to as coriander). Cilantro is a versatile ingredient in cuisines around the world. Spring is a good time to sow seeds as they thrive best during cool months; it can be grown again in fall and overwinters in mild climates. We allow a small patch to self-seed at the end of each season to emerge in late winter or early spring when conditions are favorable again. Cilantro can be winter sown in plastic jugs. Cilantro tends to bolt when summer heat sets in, which turns foliage bitter, but the flowers are a good magnet for beneficial insects. Cilantro may repel aphids, spider mites, and potato beetles.

Lavender

Lavender (*Lavandula augustifolia*) is a flowering plant in the mint family, Lamiaceae, and a native of the Mediterranean, Middle East, and India. Lavender thrives best in full sun, but it's shade tolerant. It prefers lean, well-drained soil such as a sandy loam with low to moderate fertility and does fine in slightly alkaline soil. Lavender blends well in cottage style or rock garden designs. This perennial's English varieties withstand winter temperatures to -20°F (-29°C); French lavender can tolerate around 10°F (-12°C). Lavender is another good companion plant attracting pollinators such as bees and butterflies. Lavender has antiseptic, antifungal, and anti-inflammatory properties, which may help with insect bites or minor burns. It can also assist with digestion, soothe upset stomachs, and help ease vomiting or nausea. Lavender essential oil is known to have a calming and soothing effect and lessens pain.

Lemon Balm

Lemon balm (*Melissa officinalis*) is another member of the mint family, Lamiaceae. It's native to Europe, the Mediterranean, and Central Asia, but it has naturalized throughout the globe. It is a perennial hardy to -20°F (-29°C), but it's been known to survive in climates with much lower winter temperatures with protection. I was introduced to lemon balm at our children's school where I volunteered by helping with their edible garden. I had to remove quite a few overgrown herbs, so I took home some lemon balm plants with me one year. We have those same ones, which have multiplied over the years, and which we've divided and replanted throughout our garden. Lemon balm does not grow lateral runners or rhizomes; however, it will propagate freely by seeds and can take over an area. We usually cut spent flower stalks back right away and don't leave them to seed. Over time clumps increase in size as the plants mature. Lemon balm does well in containers, which makes it easier to manage. The zesty lemony flavor of the leaves is great in hot or iced teas as well as infusing water or honey. Lemon balm possesses soothing effects that may help calm nerves or anxiety. It may boost the immune system because of its antiviral properties and antioxidant content.

Mint

Mint (*Mentha*) is another member of the mint family, Lamiaceae. We enjoy growing several varieties of mint including orange, pineapple, chocolate, ginger, grapefruit, spearmint, and banana! The different aromas and flavors add nice, refreshing flavors to ice water and teas, especially in summer. Mint is a perennial herb and thrives in full sun to part-shade depending on variety. Plant in rich, well-draining, and moderately moist soil. It's hardy to -20°F (-29°C) with some varieties able to tolerate harsher winter conditions. It's a very prolific plant with resilient rhizomes that send out runners horizontally to take over an area. Grow mint in containers to prevent spreading. A rectangular container or a window box is perfect for mint plants as these allow room for propagation, but mints are confined in their own space. Mint is known to invite pollinators if it's left to blossom. Prune spent flowers back as soon as possible to promote new growth. Mint contains phytochemicals that may help digestion, relieve flatulence and indigestion, boost immune systems, and they also have antibacterial properties. Mint may also relieve headaches and toothaches and help with cold symptoms.

Oregano

Oregano (*Origanum vulgare*) is member of the mint family, Lamiaceae, with similar growth habits as its cousins. It can be invasive when left to its own devices. Oregano is another Mediterranean native originating from Greece that's commonly used throughout the world. It grows in well-drained and moderately fertile soil and thrives in a sunny location, but it will do fine in part-sun. Oregano is a cold-hardy perennial that tolerates winter temperatures to -20°F (-29°C). It is an evergreen in temperate areas where winter temperatures fall no lower than 15°F (-9°C). Due to its vigorous nature, consider planting oregano in a container or in a framed raised bed. It tends to sprawl; keep it pruned back throughout the season. Like all herbs the best time to harvest for drying is right before the plants blossom. They usually have a higher level of essential oils during this stage making them the most fragrant and flavorful. Because of its robust aroma, oregano is excellent for culinary use. Oregano contains a powerful antioxidant that may support immune health. It's known to have anti-inflammatory, antifungal, antiviral, and anti-bacterial properties.

Parsley

Parsley (*Petroselinum crispum*) is a member of the carrot family with European origins. The pretty lacy foliage was used to season and garnish foods during ancient Greek and Roman times. Parsley is a biennial mostly grown as an annual culinary herb. The seeds are slow to germinate and may take 3–4 weeks. The plant matures between 70–90 days. If it's left in the ground for consecutive years, it will develop a flower stalk topped with umbels of tiny yellow flowers. Curly parsley tends to have a milder flavor than its counterpart (Italian parsley) and is mainly used as a garnish. Many recipes call for flat leaf or Italian parsley for its more robust and crisp taste flavoring sauces, stocks, or soups. It pairs well with savory foods such as fish and chicken.

Pineapple Sage

The gorgeous bright red and aromatic flowers of pineapple sage welcome hummingbirds and butterflies in late summer through early autumn. Pineapple sage (*Salvia elegans*) is related to mint. A tender perennial, it's generally grown as an annual in cold climates and has a cold tolerance of 20°F (-6.6°C). Protect its roots with 2–3 inches (5–7.5 cm) of organic mulch where snow is anticipated. Pineapple sage is semi-woody dwarf shrub growing to about 4 feet (1.2 m) tall and 3 feet (90 cm) wide. Plant in moist, well-drained soil in full sun. Its edible flowers and leaves are reminiscent of sweet pineapples, and they can be used to make teas and jam. The lovely blossoms are also used as garnish and in baked goods. Pineapple sage is known to have calming effects similar to mint and may aid in digestion and settle upset stomachs.

Rosemary

Smelling the fragrant foliage of the Tuscan rosemary during my morning garden walks has become habitual for me. The rich and warm scent is truly invigorating. Lightly roll its needlelike leaves between your fingers and the fragrance is dispersed into the air. Rosemary contains carnosic acid, an antioxidant that may protect the brain from free radical damage. It also possesses antibacterial, antifungal, anti-inflammatory, and antiseptic properties. Rosemary (*Rosmarinus officinalis*) is a perennial woody shrub with evergreen leaves that resemble pine needles. It blooms spring through summer with small flowers that may appear blue, white, or pink depending on variety. With its Mediterranean origins, it thrives in warm and relatively dry regions, in well-drained lean or sandy loam, and full sun. Rosemary occasionally adapts to different conditions, and most are hardy to around 15°F (-9°C). Hardier types such as 'Athens Blue Spire' (-5°F, or -20.5°C) and 'Arp' (-10°F, or -23°C) can be grown in cooler regions. Rosemary makes a great neighbor known to ward off carrot flies, cabbage moths, flies, and bean beetles.

Sage

Common sage (*Salvia officinalis*) puts on a gorgeous display of flower spikes covered with blue-violet flowers from late spring to early summer that entice bumblebees and leafcutter bees to visit. Sage is available in tricolor and purple variations, which consist of marbled pink, white, and purple shades. Sage is an evergreen woody subshrub that belongs in the mint family. It's a cold-hardy perennial to -20°F (-29°C). It prefers well-drained sandy loam soil and thrives best in full sun though it tolerates some shade. If it's been left to bloom for pollinators, cut the flower spikes back to promote foliage growth and it should flourish once more by fall. Like most vegetables and other herbs, sage has a bitter taste if it's allowed to bloom. Sage is usually used in cooked dishes as it has a pungent aroma and bold earthy flavors with hints of lemon, mint, and eucalyptus. Plant sage near vegetable crops or as a border as it's known to repel cabbage moths, carrot flies, and mosquitoes.

Sweet Cicely

Sweet cicely (*Myrrhis odorata*) is also known as sweet chervil, garden myrrh, or cicely. It is a member of the carrot family, Apiaceae. The umbels of small white flowers have similarities to parsley, cilantro, anise, and fennel blossoms. It's an eye-catching perennial with fernlike foliage and an aroma like anise. The nectar-rich clusters of tiny flowers are enjoyed by pollinators and other beneficial insects. All parts of sweet cicely are edible. The foliage and flowers can be steeped to make tea. Its white roots look like parsnips and have a delicious licorice flavor. They can be eaten raw or cooked. Sweet cicely is cold-hardy to -20°F (-29°C).

Thyme

Thyme (*Thymus vulgaris*) is a staple in many home gardens. It's a low-growing herb native to the southern area of the Mediterranean. This herbaceous perennial is cold hardy to -20°F (-29°C), although lemon thyme is only hardy to 0°F (-18°C). The leaves, growing on thin woody stems, have a pleasant aroma. Thyme is a much-loved culinary herb used to flavor vegetables, soups, meats, and fish as well as adding a savory flavor to breads. Thyme makes an attractive groundcover with its bluish-green foliage. It grows beautifully in containers with a cascading habit. I usually plant thyme on the foreground when I plant it with other Mediterranean varieties.

ABOUT THE AUTHOR

Misilla dela Llana is the host of "Learn to Grow" on YouTube where she shares practical tips and useful gardening information. Born in the Philippines as the third of five children, her family immigrated to the United States when she was ten, eventually settling in the Pacific Northwest. Misilla shares her passion for organic gardening as a tradition passed down by previous generations with her husband and their four children. For the last several years she has focused her efforts on sustainable living, homesteading, and education, sharing her experience and creating tutorials on social media platforms. In 2020, "Learn to Grow" was selected to represent Washington State for the United States of YouTube Impact. Her journey has led her to inspire others to learn how to grow food.

"Growing food sustainably and organically is essential to our future and our planet. A life lesson that we must instill in our children and future generations." -Misilla

ACKNOWLEDGMENTS

First and foremost, I would like to thank everyone on the Cool Springs Press team for all their hard work and dedication to make this book possible. Special thanks to my editor, Jessica Walliser, for all her motivation, assistance, and patience. Much appreciation to the incredible work of the creative and art team, Regina Grenier and Marissa Giambrone. Many thanks to publisher Winnie Prentiss, project managers Renae Haines, Brooke Pelletier, and managing editor John Gettings. I would like to extend my gratitude to this brilliant team at Cool Springs Press—I appreciate all your support!

Lastly, I am thankful for the constant encouragement of my loving sister, Tara Fernandez, and my dear friends Jessica Klemm and Kim Maple.

INDEX

D

K

L

M

N

O

P

R

T

U

V

W

Y